Speedwriting Shorthand

Dictionary

REVISED EDITION

Speedwriting Limited
59–60–61 South Molton Street
London W1Y 2AX

This Dictionary forms part of a complete
set of textbooks used in the tuition of
Speedwriting Shorthand. The system is
known throughout the world by the
distinguishing trade mark "Speedwriting"

ISBN 0 905480 15 5

© by Speedwriting Publishing Co. Inc. 1951, 1954, 1957

This revised edition © Speedwriting Co. Inc. and
Speedwriting Limited 1972

Reprinted 1974
1975
1976
1980

Printed in Great Britain by A. Wheaton & Co Exeter

CONTENTS

INTRODUCTION

The revision of the Speedwriting Shorthand
Dictionary was undertaken to ensure that the
content was relevant to present day needs
in the world of Commerce and to replace dated
outlines.

We would like to thank Mrs Dorothy Lipsey
and Mrs Margaret Turley for the invaluable
advice and many hours of work that they have
devoted to the task.

The outlines given in this edition of the
Dictionary are the official interpretation
as defined by Speedwriting International–London.

Shorthand outlines written by Miss Lynn Jewers

A

a		ability	
aback		abject	
abandon		abjure	
abandonment		ablative	
abase		ablaze	
abasement		able	
abash		ablution	
abate		abnegate	
abatement		abnegation	
abattoir		abnormal	
abbess		aboard	
abbey		abode	
abbot		abolish	
abbreviate		abolition	
abbreviation		abolitionist	
abdicate		abominable	
abdication		abominate	
abdomen		abomination	
abduct		aboriginal	
abduction		aborigines	
aberration		abortion	
abet		abortive	
abeyance		abound	
abhor		about	
abide		above	

1

Word	Shorthand	Word	Shorthand
abrade		abundance	
abrasion		abundant	
abrasive		abuse	(n.) / (v.)
abreast		abusive	
abridge		abut	
abroad		abyss	
abrogate		academic	
abrogation		academy	
abrupt		accede	
abruptly		accelerate	
abruptness		acceleration	
abscess		accent	
abscond		accentuate	
absence		accentuation	
absent		accept	
absolute		acceptable	
absolution		acceptance	
absolve		access	
absorb		accessible	
absorbent		accession	
absorption		accessory	
abstain		accident	
abstemious		accidental	
abstinence		acclaim	
abstract		acclamation	
abstraction		acclimatize	
absurd		acclivity	
absurdity		accommodate	

2

accommodating	*akda*	accusation	*akzy*
accommodation	*akdy*	accusative	*akzv*
accompaniment	*aco-*	accuse	*akz*
accompany	*aco*	accuser	*Akz*
accomplice	*akps*	accustom	*aksn*
accomplish	*akpʒ*	ace	*as*
accomplishment	*akpʒ-*	acerbity	*asb)*
accord	*ak/*	acetic	*as⊤*
accordance	*ak//*	acetylene	*aslln*
accordant	*ak/-*	ache	*ak*
according	*ak/*	achieve	*ace*
accordingly	*ak/e*	achievement	*ace-*
accordion	*ak/n*	acid	*asd*
accost	*ak,*	acidity	*asd)*
account	*akl*	acknowledge	*ak*
accountable	*aklb*	acknowledgment	*ak-*
accountant	*akl-*	acme	*akn,*
accoutrements	*all--*	acorn	*akn*
accredit	*acr*	acoustic	*akS*
accretion	*aky*	acquaint	*aq-*
accrue	*aku*	acquaintance	*aq-'*
accumulate	*akla*	acquiescence	*aqs/*
accumulating	*akla*	acquiescent	*aqs-*
accumulation	*akly*	acquire	*aqu*
accumulative	*aklv*	acquisition	*aqzy*
accumulator	*Akla*	acquisitive	*aqzv*
accuracy	*akus,*	acquit	*aql*
accurate	*akua*	acquittal	*aqll*

3

Word	Shorthand	Word	Shorthand
acre	*Uk*	addendum	*ad —*
acrimonious	*aknx*	adder	*ad*
acrimony	*akn,*	addition	*ady*
acrobat	*akbl*	additional	*adyl*
acrobatic	*akb'*	addict	*adk*
acropolis	*akpls*	address	*ad'*
across	*ak'*	adept	*adp*
act	*ak*	adequacy	*adqs,*
acting	*ak*	adequate	*adqa*
action	*aky*	adhere	*adhe*
actionable	*akyb*	adherence	*adhe/*
active	*akv*	adherent	*adhe -*
activity	*akv)*	adhesion	*adhy*
actor	*Uk*	adieu	*adu*
actress	*ak'*	adipose	*adpz*
actual	*akl*	adjacent	*ajs -*
actuary	*aky*	adjective (adj)	*ajkv*
actuate	*aka*	adjoin	*ayyn*
acumen	*akn*	adjourn	*ayun*
acute	*aku*	adjudge	*ay*
adage	*ady*	adjudicate	*aydka*
adamant	*adn -*	adjudication	*aydky*
adamantine	*adn - un*	adjudicator	*aydka*
adapt	*adp*	adjunct	*ayq*
adaptable	*adpb*	adjure	*ayu*
adaptability	*adpb)*	adjust	*ay,*
adaptation	*adpy*	adjustment	*ays -*
add	*ad*	adjutant	*ayl -*

4

Word	Shorthand	Word	Shorthand
administer		adulterate	
administrate		adulteration	
administrator		adulterator	
admirable		adultery	
admiral		advance	
admiration		advancement	
admire		advantage	
admirer		advantageous	
admissible		advent	
admission		adventitious	
admit		adventure	
admittance		adventurer	
admixture		adventuresome	
admonish		adventurous	
admonition		adverb (adv)	
ado		adversary	
adolescence		adverse	
adopt		adversity	
adoption		advertise	
adorable		advertisement	
adoration		advertiser	
adore		advice	
adorn		advisable	
adornment		advise	
adroit		adviser	
adulation		advocacy	
adulatory		advocate	
adult		adze	

5

Word	Outline	Word	Outline
aerate		afforestation	
aeration		affray	
aerial		affright	
aerie		affront	
aeriform		afield	
aerodrome		afire	
aeronaut		aflame	
aeronautics		afloat	
aeroplane		afoot	
aesthetic		afore	
afar		aforesaid	
affable		afraid	
affair		afresh	
affect		Africa	
affectation		aft	
affection		after	
affectionate		aftermath	
affiance		aftermost	
affidavit		afternoon	
affiliate		afterthought	
affinity		afterwards	
affirm		again	
affix		against	
afflict		agape	
affliction		agate	
affluence		age	
affluent		aged	
afford		agency	

6

English	Shorthand	English	Shorthand
agent (agt)		aim	
age-old		air	
agglomerate		airy	
agglutinate		aisle	
aggravate		ajar	
aggravation		akimbo	
aggregate		akin	
aggregation		alabaster	
aggression		alacrity	
aggressive		alarm	
aggressor		alarmist	
aggrieve		alas	
aghast		alb	
agile		albatross	
agitate		albeit	
aglow		albino	
ago		album	
agony		albumen	
agree		alchemy	
agreeable		alcohol	
agreement		alcoholic	
agricultural		alcove	
agriculture		alderman	
aground		ale	
ague		alert	
ahead		algebra (alg)	
aid		alias	
ail		alibi	

7

alien		allowable	
alienate		allowance	
alienist		alloy	
alight		allude	
align		allure	
alignment		allusion	
alike		allusive	
alimentary		alluvial	
alimony		alluvium	
alive		ally	
alkali		almanac	
alkaline		almighty	
all		almond	
allay		almost	
allegation		alms	
allege		aloes	
allegiance		aloft	
allegory		alone	
alleviate		along	
alley		alongside	
alliance		aloof	
allied		aloud	
alligator		alp	
alliteration		alphabet	
allocate		alpine	
allot		already	
allotment		also	
allow		altar	

8

alter		ambitious	
alteration		amble	
altercate		ambush	
altercation		ameliorate	
alternate		amelioration	
alternation		ameliorative	
alternative		amen	
although		amenable	
altitude		amend	
alto		amendment	
altogether		amenity	
alum		America	
aluminium		American	
always		Americanization	
am		amiability	
amalgam		amiable	
amalgamate		amicable	
amalgamation		amid	
amass		amidst	
amateur		amiss	
amatory		amity	
amaze		ammonia	
amazement		ammunition	
ambassador		amnesia	
amber		amnesty	
ambiguity		amnesties	
ambiguous		among	
ambition		amongst	

9

Word	Outline	Word	Outline
amorous		anarchy	
amorphous		anathema	
amortize		anatomical	
amount		anatomy	
ampere		ancestor	
amphibious		anchor	
amphitheatre		anchorage	
ample		anchovy	
amplification		ancient	
amplify		and	
amplitude		andante	
amputate		anecdote	
amulet		anemone	
amuse		anew	
amusement		angel	
an		angelic	
anachronism		anger	
anaemia		angle	
anaesthetic		Anglian	
anagram		Anglican	
analogous		angrily	
analogy		angry	
analyse		anguish	
analysis		animadversion	
analyst		animadvert	
analytic		animal	
analytical		animate	
anarchist		animation	

10

animosity		anonymity	
aniseed		anonymous	
ankle		anonymously	
annal		another	
annalist		answer	
anneal		ant	
annex		antagonism	
annihilate		antagonist	
annihilation		antagonistic	
anniversary		antagonize	
annotate		antarctic	
annotation		antecedent	
announce		antechamber	
announcement		antedate	
annoy v. 口语		antediluvian	
annoyance		antelope	
annual		antemeridian	
annuitant		antenna	
annuity		antennae	
annul		anterior	
annunciate		anteroom	
annunciation		anthem	
anode		anthology	
anodyne		anthracite	
anoint		anthrax	
anomalous		anthropological	
anomaly		anthropology	
anon		anti	

11

Word	Shorthand	Word	Shorthand
antic	a-k	anywhere	n, ⌣ɾ
Antichrist	a-k,	aorta	a/a
antichristian	a-ksn	apace	aps
anticipant	a-sp-	apart	ap/
anticipate	a-spa	apartment (apt)	ap/-
anticipation	a-spy	apathetic	apl⊤
anticlimax	a-klᴍx	apathy	apl,
antidote	a-do	ape	ap
antipathy	a-pl,	aperient	aP-
antiquary	a-qy	aperture	aplu
antiquate	a-qa	apex	apx
antiquated	a-qā	aphorism	afʒ⌢
antique	a-k	apiary	apy
antiquity	a-q)	apiece	aps
antiseptic	a-spk	apocalypse	apklps
antithesis	a-lss	apologetic	apol⊤
antithetical	a-ttK	apologize	apolʒ
antitoxin	a-lxn	apology	apol
antler	a-l	apoplexy	appx,
anvil	avl	apostasy	apss,
anxiety	ax)	apostate	apsa
anxious	ax	apostle	apsl
any	n,	apostolic	apslk
anybody	n, bd,	apostrophe	apsf,
anyhow	n, h⌣	apothecary	aplky
anyone	n, ı	apotheosis	aplss
anything	n₂	appal	apl
anyway	n, ⌣a	appalling	apl̲

12

Word	Shorthand	Word	Shorthand
apparatus		apposition	
apparel		appraise	
apparent		appreciable	
apparition		appreciate	
appeal		appreciation	
appear		appreciative	
appearance		apprehend	
appease		apprehension	
appellant		apprehensive	
appellation		apprentice	
append		apprize	
appendicitis		approach	
appendix		approachable	
appertain		approbation	
appetite		appropriate	
applaud		appropriation	
applause		approval	
apple		approve	
appliance		approximate	
applicability		approximately	
applicable		approximation	
applicant		appurtenance	
application		apricot	
applied		April	
apply		apron	
appoint		apropos	
appointment		apse	
apportion		apt	

13

Word	Shorthand	Word	Shorthand
aptitude	*(shorthand)*	are	*(shorthand)*
aqua	*(shorthand)*	area	*(shorthand)*
aquamarine	*(shorthand)*	arena	*(shorthand)*
aquarelle	*(shorthand)*	aren't	*(shorthand)*
aquarium	*(shorthand)*	arguable	*(shorthand)*
aquatic	*(shorthand)*	argue	*(shorthand)*
aqueduct	*(shorthand)*	argument	*(shorthand)*
aquiline	*(shorthand)*	argumentative	*(shorthand)*
arable	*(shorthand)*	arid	*(shorthand)*
arbiter	*(shorthand)*	aright	*(shorthand)*
arbitrary	*(shorthand)*	arise	*(shorthand)*
arbitrate	*(shorthand)*	aristocracy	*(shorthand)*
arbitration	*(shorthand)*	aristocrat	*(shorthand)*
arboretum	*(shorthand)*	aristocratic	*(shorthand)*
arbour	*(shorthand)*	arithmetic (arith)	*(shorthand)*
arc	*(shorthand)*	ark	*(shorthand)*
arch	*(shorthand)*	arm	*(shorthand)*
archaeology	*(shorthand)*	armament	*(shorthand)*
archaic	*(shorthand)*	armature	*(shorthand)*
archbishop	*(shorthand)*	armful	*(shorthand)*
archer	*(shorthand)*	armhole	*(shorthand)*
archipelago	*(shorthand)*	armistice	*(shorthand)*
architect	*(shorthand)*	armour	*(shorthand)*
architecture	*(shorthand)*	armorial	*(shorthand)*
archway	*(shorthand)*	army	*(shorthand)*
arctic	*(shorthand)*	aroma	*(shorthand)*
ardent	*(shorthand)*	aromatic	*(shorthand)*
ardour	*(shorthand)*	arose	*(shorthand)*

14

Word	Shorthand	Word	Shorthand
around	ᴦᴗ	artisan	a/ȝn
arouse	ɑᴦ₃	artist	a/,
arraign	ɑᴦn	artistic	a/S
arrange	ɑᴦy	artless	a/ℓ'
arrangement	ɑᴦy-	as	as
arrant	ɑᴦ-	asbestos	asbss
array	ɑᴦa	ascend	as —
arrear	ɑᴦe	ascension	asy
arrest	ɑᴦ,	ascent	as-
arrestment	ɑᴦs-	ascertain	asln
arrival	ᴦvl	ascribe	askb
arrive	ᴦv	ash	aȝ
arrogance	ɑᴦg/	ashamed	aȝā
arrogant	ɑᴦg-	ashore	aȝo
arrow	ɑᴦo	Asia	aȝa
arsenal	asnl	aside	asd
arsenic	asnk	ask	sk
arson	asn	askance	ask/
art	a/	askew	asku
artery	a/y	aslant	asl-
artful	a/f	asleep	aslp
artichoke	a/ck	asp	as
article (art)	a/K	asparagus	asᵖgx
articulate	a/kla	aspect	ask
articulation	a/kly	aspen	asn
artifice	a/fs	asperity	as)
artificial	a/fx	aspersion	asy
artillery	a/ly	asphalt	asfll

aspirate		association	
aspiration		assort	
aspire		assortment	
ass		assuage	
assail		assume	
assailant		assumption	
assassinate		assurance	
assault		assure	
assay		assuredly	
assemblage		aster	
assemble		asterisk	
assembly		astern	
assent		asteroid	
assert		asthma	
assertion		asthmatic	
assess		astonish	
assessment		astonishment	
assets		astound	
assiduous		astral	
assign		astray	
assignation		astride	
assignment		astringent	
assimilate		astrology	
assist		astronomy	
assistance		astute	
assistant		astuteness	
assize		asunder	
associate		asylum	

16

Word	Shorthand	Word	Shorthand
at		attic	
ate		attire	
atheism		attitude	
atheist		attorney	
athlete		attract	
athletic		attraction	
Atlantic		attractive	
atmosphere		attribute	
atom		attribution	
atone		attributive	
atonement		auburn	
atrocious		auction	
atrocity		auctioneer	
attach		audacious	
attachment		audacity	
attack		audible	
attain		audience	
attainable		audit	
attainment		auditor	
attempt		auditorium	
attend		auditory	
attendance		aught	
attendant		augment	
attention		augmentation	
attentive		augur	
attenuate		August	
attest		aunt	
attestation		auricle	

17

English	Shorthand	English	Shorthand
auricular		autumnal	
aurist		auxiliary	
aurora		avail	
auspicious		available	
austere		avalanche	
austerity		avarice	
Australia		avaricious	
authentic		avenge	n. 復仇, 報復
authenticate		avenger	
authenticity		avenue	
author		aver	
authoress		average	
authoritative		averse	
authority		aversion	
authorization		avert	
authorize		aviary	
autobiography		aviation	
autocracy		aviator	
autocrat		avid	
autograph		avoid	
automatic		avoidable	
automation		avoidance	
automaton		avoirdupois	
automobile		avow	
autonomous		avowal	n. 聲言, 供認
autonomy		avowedly	ad. 公然
autopsy		await	
autumn		awake	v. 喚起

18

awaken	a‑kn	awning	an
award	a/	awoke	a‑k
aware	a‑a	awry	aru
away	a‑a	axe	ax
awe	a	axiom	x‑
awful	af	axis	xs
awhile	a‑l	axle	xl
awkward	ak/	azure	az/
awl	al		

B

babble	bb	bait	ba
baboon	bbn	baize	bз
baby	bb,	bake	bk
bachelor	Bcl	baker	Bk
back	bk	balance	bal
backbone	bkbn	balcony	blk,
backer	Bk	bald	bald
backward	bk/	baldness	bld'
bacon	bkn	bale	bal
bad	bd	balk	bak
badge	bɟ	ball	bal
badger	Bɟ	ballad	bld
badness	bd'	ballast	bl,
baffle	bfl	ballet	bla
bag	bq	balloon	bln
baggage	bɟ	ballot	bll
bail	bal	balm	b‑

19

Word	Shorthand	Word	Shorthand
balsam		bar	
baluster		barb	
balustrade		barbarian	
bamboo		barbarous	
ban		barber	
banal		barbican	
banana		bard	
band		bare	
bandage		barefaced	
bandit		barefoot	
bandy		bareness	
bane		bargain	
bang		barge	
bangle		baritone	
banish		bark	
banishment		barley	
banister		barn	
banjo		barnacle	
bank		barnyard	
banker		barometer	
bankrupt		baron	
bankruptcy		baroness	
banner		barouche	
banquet		barrack	
banter		barrage	
baptism		barrel	
Baptist		barren	
baptize		barricade	

20

Word	Shorthand	Word	Shorthand
barrier		baton	
barrister		batsman	
barrow		battalion	
barter		batten	
base		batter	
baseball		battery	
basement		battle	
baseness		battlement	
bashful		battleship	
bashfulness		bauble	
basic		bawl	
basin		bay	
basis		bayonet	
bask		bazaar	
basket		be	
bass		beach	
bastard		beacon	
baste		bead	
basting		beading	
bastion		beadle	
bat		beagle	
batch		beak	
bate		beam	
bath		bean	
bathe		beanstalk	
bathrobe		bear	
bathroom		beard	
batiste		bearer	

Word	Outline	Word	Outline
bearing	ba	bedtime	bdli
beast ✓	be,	bee	be
beastliness	bsl'	beech	bec
beastly	bsl	beef	bef
beat	be	been	b
beaten	ben	beer	be
beater	Be	beet	be
beating	be	beetle	bll
beau	bo	befall	bfl
beauteous	blx	befell	bfl
beautiful	blf	before	bf
beautifully	blf	beforehand	bfh—
beautify	blf	befriend	bf—
beauty	bl,	beg	bg
beaver	Bv	began	bgn
became	bk	beget	bgl
because	ks	beggar	Bg
beck	bk	beggarly	Bgl
beckon	bkn	begin	bg
become	bk	beginner	Bg
bed	bd	begrudge	bgj
bedchamber	bdCb	beguile	bgl
bedding	bd	begun	bgn
bedlam	bdl	behalf	bhf
bedridden	bdrdn	behave	bha
bedroom	bdr	behaviour	Bha
bedspread	bdsd	behead	bhd
bedstead	bdsd	beheld	bhl

22

Word	Shorthand	Word	Shorthand
behind	*bh—*	benefice	*bnfs*
behold	*bhol*	beneficent	*bnfs-*
being	*b*	beneficial	*bnfx*
belabour	*blab*	beneficiary	*bnffy*
belated	*blā*	benefit	*bnf*
belch	*blc*	benevolence	*bnvl/*
beleaguer	*blg*	benevolent	*bnvl-*
belfry	*blf,*	benighted	*bnī*
belie	*bli*	benign	*bnin*
belief	*blf*	bent	*b-*
believe	*ble*	benzine	*bnzn*
believer	*Ble*	bequeath	*bql*
bell	*bl*	bereave	*bre*
belle	*bl.*	bereavement	*bre-*
belligerent	*blj-*	bereft	*brf*
bellow	*blo*	berry	*by*
belly	*bl,*	berth	*brl*
belong	*blg*	beseech	*bsc*
beloved	*blṽ*	beset	*bsl*
below	*blo*	beside	*bsd*
belt	*bll*	besides	*bsds*
bemoan	*brn*	besiege	*bsy*
bench	*bc*	besotted	*bsī*
bend	*b—*	besought	*bsl*
beneath	*bnl*	bespatter	*bSa*
benediction	*bndky*	bespeak	*bsk*
benefactor	*bnJk*	best	*b,*
benefactress	*bnfk'*	bestial	*bsl*

bestir		bibliography	
bestow		bibulous	
bestride		biceps	
bet		bicker	
betake		bicycle	
betide		bid	
betimes		bide	
betook		biennial	
betray		bier	
betrayal		big	
betroth		bigamous	
betrothal		bigamy	
betrothed		bigger	
better		biggest	
between		bight	
betwixt		bigness	
bevel		bigot	
beverage		bigotry	
bevy		bile	
bewail		bilious	
beware		bill	
bewildered		billet	
bewilderment		billiards	
bewitch		billion	
bey		billow	
beyond		bin	
bias		bind	
bible		binder	

binds		blackberry	
binomial		blackbird	
biography		blackboard	
biographical		blacken	
biology		blackness	
birch		blacksmith	
bird		blackthorn	
birth		blackguard	
birthday		bladder	
birthplace		blade	
birthright		blame	
biscuit		blameless	
bisect		blanch	
bisector		bland	
bishop		blandishment	
bishopric		blank	
bismuth		blanket	
bison		blare	
bit		blaspheme	
bitch		blasphemy	
bite		blast	
bitter		blasting	
bitterness		blatant	
bitumen		blaze	
bituminous		blazon	
bivalve		bleach	
bivouac		bleak	
black		bleaker	

Word	Outline	Word	Outline
blear		bloody	
bleat		bloom	
bled		bloomer	
bleed		blossom	
blemish		blot	
blend		blouse	
bless		blow	
blessedness		blower	
blessing		blubber	
blest		bludgeon	
blew		blue	
blight		bluebell	
blind		bluebird	
blindly		bluff	
blindness		bluish	
blink		blunder	
bliss		blunt	
blissful		blur	
blister		blurred	
blithe		blush	
blizzard		bluster	
bloat		boa	
block		boar	
blockade		board	
blockhead		boarder	
blond		boardroom	
blood		boast	
bloodshed		boastful	

boat	‌	bonnet	‌
boatman	‌	bonny	‌
boatswain	‌	bonus	‌
bob	‌	book	‌
bobbin	‌	bookcase	‌
bode	‌	book-keeping	‌
bodice	‌	booklet	‌
bodily	‌	boom	‌
bodkin	‌	boon	‌
body	‌	boor	‌
bodyguard	‌	boorish	‌
bog	‌	boost	‌
boil	‌	boot	‌
boiler	‌	booth	‌
boisterous	‌	booty	‌
bold	‌	borax	‌
boldness	‌	border	‌
bolster	‌	bore	‌
bolt	‌	boredom	‌
bomb	‌	boric	‌
bombard	‌	born	‌
bombardment	‌	borne	‌
bombast	‌	borough	‌
bona fide	‌	borrow	‌
bond	‌	borrower	‌
bondage	‌	bosom	‌
bone	‌	boss	‌
bonfire	‌	botanical	‌

Word	Shorthand	Word	Shorthand
botanist		boxer	
botany		boxroom	
botch		boy	
both		boycott	
bother		boyhood	
bottle		boyish	
bottom		brace	
bottomless		bracelet	
bough		bracket	
bought		brag	
boulder		braggart	
boulevard		braid	
bounce		brail	
bound		brain	
boundary		brake	
boundless		bramble	
boundlessness		bran	
bounteous		branch	
bountiful		brand	
bounty		brandish	
bouquet		brandy	
bout		brass	
bow		brassiere	
bowels		bravado	
bower		brave	
bowl		bravery	
bowler		bravo	
box		brawl	

28

brawn		brew	
brawny		brewer	
bray		brewery	
brazen		briar	
breach		bribe	
bread		brick	
breadth		bridal	
break		bride	
breakable		bridegroom	
breaker		bridge	
breakfast		bridle	
breakwater		brief	
breast		brigade	
breastplate		brigadier	
breath		brigand	
breathe		bright	
breathless		brighten	
bred		brighter	
breech		brightly	
breeches		brightness	
breed		brilliancy	
breeding		brilliant	
breeze		brim	
breezy		brimstone	
brethren		brindled	
brevet		brine	
breviary		bring	
brevity		brink	

brisk		brotherhood	
bristle		brotherly	
Britain		brougham	
British		brought	
brittle		brow	
broach		brown	
broad		brownie	
broadcast		browse	
broaden		bruise	
broader		brunette	
broadly		brunt	
broadness		brush	
broadsword		brushwood	
brocade		brutal	
brochure		brutality	
broil		brutalize	
broke		brute	
broken		bubble	
broker		buccaneer	
brokerage		buck	
bronchitis		bucket	
bronze		buckle	
brooch		buckler	
brood		buckram	
brook		bud	
broom		budge	
broth		budget	
brother		buff	

30

Word	Shorthand	Word	Shorthand
buffalo	*bflo*	bungalow	*bglo*
buffer	*bf*	bungle	*bgl*
buffet	*bfa*	bunion	*bnn*
buffoon	*bfn*	bunting	*b=*
bug	*bg*	buoy	*by*
buggy	*bg,*	buoyancy	*by/*
bugle	*bgl*	buoyant	*by–*
build	*bld*	burden	*b/n*
builder	*Bld*	bureau	*buo*
building	*bldg* (n.)	burgess	*by'*
built	*bll*	burglar	*Brgl*
bulb	*blb*	burial	*byl*
bulbous	*blbx*	buried	*bȳ*
bulk	*blk*	burlesque	*brlsk*
bulky	*blk,*	burly	*brl*
bull	*bl*	burn	*brn*
bullet	*bll*	burner	*Brn*
bulletin	*blln*	burnish	*brnʒ*
bullion	*bln*	burrow	*bro*
bullock	*blk*	bursar	*Brs*
bully	*bl,*	bursary	*brsy*
bulwark	*bl–rk*	burst	*br,*
bump	*b⌐p*	bury	*by*
bumper	*B⌐p*	bus	*bs*
bun	*bn*	bush	*bʒ*
bunch	*bc*	bushel	*bʒl*
bundle	*b_l*	bushy	*bʒ,*
bung	*bg*	busier	*Bʒ*

31

busily	*bzl*	butterfly	*Bfl*
business	*bs*	button	*btn*
busk	*bsk*	buttress	*bt'*
bust	*b,*	buxom	*bx*
bustle	*bsl*	buy	*b*
busy	*b3*	buyer	*B*
but	*b*	buzz	*b3*
butcher	*Bc*	buzzard	*b3/*
butler	*Bll*	by	*b*
butter	*B*	bye	*b*
buttercup	*Bkp*		

C

cab	*kb*	cake	*kk*
cabalistic	*kbS*	calamitous	*klx*
cabbage	*kbj*	calamity	*kl)*
cabin	*kbn*	calculate	*klkla*
cabinet	*kbnl*	calculation	*klklj*
cable	*kb*	calculus	*klllx*
cackle	*kK*	calendar	*Kl*
cadaverous	*kDvx*	calf	*kf*
caddie	*kd,*	calibre	*Klb*
cadence	*kd/*	calico	*klko*
cadet	*kdl*	call	*kl*
cafe	*kfa*	caller	*Kl*
cafeteria	*kflya*	callous	*klx*
cage	*kaj*	callow	*klo*
cajole	*kjl*	calm	*k*

Word	Shorthand	Word	Shorthand
calmness		candidacy	
calomel		candidate	
caloric		candle	
calorific		candlestick	
calumnious		candour	
calumny		candy	
calves		cane	
calyx		canine	
cambric		canister	
came		canker	
camel		cankerous	
cameo		canned	
camera		canner	
camomile		cannery	
camouflage		cannibal	
camp		cannibalism	
campaign		cannibalistic	
camper		cannon	
camphor		cannot	
campus		canny	
can		canoe	
canal		canon	
canary		canonical	
cancel		canopy	
cancellation		can't	
cancer		cantaloupe	
cancerous		canteen	
candid		canter	

Word	Shorthand	Word	Shorthand
cantilever	k-le	captive	kpv
canton	k-n	captivity	kpv)
canvas	kvs	capture	kpu
canyon	kyn	car	ka
cap	kp	caramel	krl
capability	kpb)	carat	krl
capable	kpb	caravan	krvn
capacious	kpsc	carbine	kabn
capacitate	kpsla	carbohydrate	kabHa
capacity	kps)	carbolic	kablk
cape	kap	carbon	kabn
caper	Kp	carbonic	kabnk
capillary	kply	carboniferous	kabnfsc
capital	kpll	carbonize	kabnz
capitalism	kpllz	carbuncle	kabgl
capitalist	kpll,	carburation	kaby
capitation	kply	carburetter	Kabr
capitulate	kplla	carcass	kak'
capitulation	kplly	card	k/
capon	kpn	cardboard	k/b/
caprice	kps	cardiac	k/k
capricious	kpsc	cardinal	k/rl
capriciousness	kpsc'	care	ka
capsize	kpsz	career	kre
capsule	kpsl	careful	kaf
captain	kpn	carefully	kaf
caption	kpy	carefulness	kaf'
captivate	kpva	careless	kal'

34

carelessness	*ka"*	cartridge	*k/₁*
caress	*kr'*	carve	*krv*
caret	*krl*	cascade	*kskd*
cargo	*kaq*	cascara	*kskra*
caricature	*krklu*	case	*kas*
carnage	*kary*	case-hardened	*ksh/n̄*
carnal	*karl*	casement	*ks-*
carnation	*kary*	cash	*k3*
carnival	*karvl*	cash-book	*k3bk*
carnivorous	*kaNvx*	cashier	*k3e*
carol	*krl*	cashmere	*k3re*
carouse	*kr_z*	casket	*kskl*
carpenter	*Kap-*	casque	*ksk*
carpentry	*kap-,*	casserole	*ksl*
carpet	*kapl*	cassock	*ksk*
carriage	*kry*	cast	*k,*
carrier	*Ky*	castigate	*ksga*
carrion	*kyn*	castigation	*ksgl*
carrot	*krl*	castle	*ksl*
carry	*ky*	castor	*k9*
cart	*k/*	castrate	*k9a*
cartage	*k/₁*	casual	*kzl*
carter	*K/*	casualties	*kzll,,*
cartilage	*k/l*	casualty	*kzll,*
cartographer	*K/gl*	casuist	*kzu,*
cartography	*k/gl,*	cat	*kl*
cartoon	*k/n*	catacomb	*klku*
cartoonist	*k/n,*	catalogue	*cal*

Word	Shorthand	Word	Shorthand
catapult	klpll	cease	ses
cataract	Klk	ceaseless	ssl'
catarrh	kla	cedar	Se
catastrophe	klSf,	cede	sd
catch	kc	ceiling	slq
catechism	klkz	celebrate	slba
catechize	klkz	celebration	slby
categorical	klgrK	celebrity	slb)
category	klgy	celerity	slr)
cater	Ka	celery	sly
cathedral	kldl	celestial	slsl
catkin	klkn	celibacy	slbs,
cattle	kll	cell	sl
caucus	kkx	cellar	Sl
caught	kal	celluloid	sllyd
cauldron	kldn	cellulose	slls
cauliflower	klfl	cement	s-
cause	kz	cemetery	s~ly
caustic	kS	cenotaph	snlf
cauterize	Klz	censer	S/
caution	ky	censor	S/
cautious	kx	censorious	S/yx
cavalcade	kvlkd	censorship	S/3
cavalier	kvle	censure	S/u
cavalry	kvlr,	census	S/x
cave	ka	cent	c
cavern	kvrn	centenary	s- ny
cavity	kv)	centennial	s-nl

36

Word	Shorthand	Word	Shorthand
central		challenge	
centralization		challenger	
centralize		chamber	
centre		chamberlain	
centrifugal		chambermaid	
century		chameleon	
cereal		chamois	
cerebellum		champ	
cerebral		champagne	
ceremonial		champion	
ceremonious		championship	
ceremony		chance	
certain		chancel	
certainty		chancellor	
certificate (cert)		chancery	
certify		chances	
certitude		chandelier	
cessation		chandler	
cesspool		change	
chafe		changeable	
chaff		channel	
chaffinch		chant	
chagrin		chaos	
chain		chaotic	
chair		chap	
chairman		chapel	
chalice		chaperon	
chalk		chaplain	

chaplet	*cpl*	chat	*cl*
chapter	*Cp*	chateau	*Zlo*
chapterhouse	*Cph̬s*	chattels	*clls*
char	*ca*	chatter	*Cl*
character	*Krk*	chauffeur	*Zfr*
characteristic	*KrkS*	chauffeuse	*Zfz*
characterize	*Krkz*	cheap	*cep*
charade	*Zrd*	cheapen	*cpn*
charcoal	*crkl*	cheat	*ce*
charge	*cq*	check	*ck*
chargeable	*cgb*	checkmate	*ckra*
charger	*Cq*	cheek	*cek*
chariot	*cyl*	cheer	*ce*
charioteer	*cyle*	cheerful	*cef*
charitable	*crlb*	cheerfulness	*cef'*
charity	*cr)*	cheerily	*cel*
charlatan	*Zrlln*	cheerless	*cel'*
charm	*crᴗ*	cheery	*ce,*
chart	*c/*	cheese	*c3*
charter	*C/*	chemical	*kᴗK*
chary	*cy*	chemise	*Zᴗ3*
chase	*cas*	chemist	*kᴗ,*
chasm	*kzᴗ*	chemistry	*kᴗᏸ,*
chaste	*ca,*	cheque	*ck*
chasten	*csn*	chequer	*Ck*
chastise	*csᴈ*	cherish	*crᏸ*
chastisement	*csᴈ-*	cherry	*cy*
chastity	*cs)*	cherub	*crb*

Word	Outline	Word	Outline
cherubim		chin	
chess		china	
chest		Chinese	
chestnut		chink	
chew		chintz	
chicanery		chip	
chick		chiropodist	
chicken		chirp	
chicory		chisel	
chide		chivalrous	
chief		chivalry	
chiefly		chive	
chieftain		chocolate	
chiffon		choice	
chiffonier		choir	
child		choke	
childhood		cholera	
childish		choleric	
childless		choose	
childlike		chop	
children		chopper	
chill		choral	
chilliness		chord	
chilly		chorister	
chime		chorus	
chimer		chose	
chimera		christen	
chimney		Christian	

39

Word	Shorthand	Word	Shorthand
Christianity		cipher	
Christmas (Xmas)		circle	
chromatic		circlet	
chronic		circuit	
chronicle		circuitous	
chronologist		circular	
chronology		circulate	
chronometer		circulation	
chrysalis		circumcise	
chrysanthemum		circumcision	
chubby		circumference	
chuck		circumflex	
chuckle		circumlocution	
chum		circumlocutory	
church		circumnavigate	
churchman		circumnavigation	
churchyard		circumnavigator	
churl		circumscribe	
churlish		circumscription	
churn		circumspect	
chute		circumspection	
cider		circumspectly	
cigar		circumstance	
cigarette		circumstances	
cinch		circumstantial	
cinder		circumvent	
cinema		circus	
cinnamon		cirrus	

English	Shorthand	English	Shorthand
cist	*s,*	clapper	*Kp*
cistern	*sᴧn*	claret	*krl*
citadel	*sldl*	clarification	*krf*
citation	*siy*	clarify	*krf*
cite	*sı*	clarion	*krn*
citizen	*slzn*	clarity	*kr)*
city (C)	*s)*	clash	*kʃ*
civic	*svk*	clasp	*ks*
civil	*svl*	class	*k'*
civilian	*svln*	classic	*ksk*
civility	*svl)*	classical	*ksk*
civilization	*svlzy*	classification	*ksf*
civilize	*svlz*	classify	*ksf*
clad	*kd*	classmate	*ksↄa*
claim	*ka*	clatter	*Ka*
claimant	*ka-*	clause	*kz*
clam	*kↄ*	claw	*ka*
clamber	*Knↄ*	clay	*ka*
clammy	*kↄ,*	clean	*kn*
clamorous	*Knx*	cleaner	*Kn*
clamour	*Kↄ*	cleanliness	*knl'*
clamp	*kↄp*	cleanse	*knz*
clan	*kn*	clear	*ke*
clandestine	*k — sn*	clearance	*ke/*
clang	*kg*	clearness	*ke'*
clank	*kq*	cleavage	*kej*
clannish	*knʃ*	cleave	*ke*
clap	*kp*	cleaver	*Ke*

clef		cloister	
cleft		close	
clemency		close (verb)	
clement		closed	
clench		closeness	
clergy		closer	
clergyman		closet	
clerk		clot	
clever		cloth	
click		clothe	
client		clothes	
clientele		clothing	
cliff		cloud	
climate		cloudless	
climax		cloudy	
climb		clout	
clinch		clove	
cling		cloven	
clinic		clover	
clinical		clown	
clink		cloy	
clinker		club	
clip		clump	
cloak		clumsy	
clock		clung	
clockmaker		cluster	
clod		clutch	
clog		coach	

Word	Shorthand	Word	Shorthand
coachman	*ke͞n_*	coerce	*kors*
coadjutor	*kaju*	coercion	*koj*
coagulate	*kgla*	coexist	*kxc,*
coagulation	*kglj*	coffee	*kfe*
coal	*kol*	coffer	*kf*
coalesce	*kls*	coffin	*kfn*
coalescence	*klsv*	cog	*kg*
coalition	*klj*	cogent	*kj_*
coarse	*kors*	cogitate	*kjla*
coarseness	*kors'*	cogitation	*kjlj*
coast	*ko,*	cognate	*kgna*
coat	*ko*	cognition	*kgnj*
coax	*kox*	cognizance	*kgnz/*
cob	*kb*	cognizant	*kgnz_*
cobble	*kb*	cognomen	*kgnm*
cobbler	*Kb*	cohere	*khe*
cobweb	*kbb*	coherent	*khe_*
cocaine	*kkn*	cohesion	*khj*
cock	*kk*	cohesive	*khsv*
cockade	*kkd*	cohort	*kh/*
cockle	*kK*	coif	*gf*
cocktail	*kkll*	coiffure	*gfu*
cocoa	*kko*	coil	*kyl*
coconut	*kknl*	coin	*kyn*
cocoon	*kkn*	coinage	*kynj*
cod	*kd*	coincide	*knsd*
coddle	*kdl*	coincidence	*knsd/*
code	*kd*	coincident	*knsd_*

coke	kok	coloration	Klɉ
colander	Kl __	colour	Kl
cold	kol	colourless	Kll'
colder	Kol	colt	koll
coldness	hol'	column	hl
colic	klk	coma	kʌa
collapse	klps	comb	ko
collar	Kl	combat	hbl
collate	kla	combatant	kbl-
collateral	kʌll	combative	kbv
collation	klɉ	combination	kbny
colleague	klg	combine	kbʌ
collect	kk	combustible	kbsb
collection	kky	combustion	kbsy
collective	kkv	come	k
college	klɉ	comedian	kdn
collegiate	klɉa	comedy	kd,
collide	kld	comeliness	kl'
collier	Kl,	comely	kl
colliery	kly	comer	K
collision	klɉ	comet	kl
Cologne	kln	comfort	kɉ/
colon	kln	comfortable	kɉ/b
colonel	col	comfortably	kɉ/b
colonial	klnl	comforter	Kɉ/
colonist	kln,	comfortless	kɉ/l'
colonize	klnz	comical	kK
colony	kln,	coming	k

44

Word	Shorthand	Word	Shorthand
comma	ka	commodity	kd)
command	k __	commodore	kdo
commandant	k __ _	common	kn
commander	K __	commoner	Kn n. ƚ̶ɓ
commemorate	k⌣ra	commonly	knl
commemoration	k⌣ry	commonplace	knpl
commemorative	k⌣rv	commonwealth	knll
commence	k/	commotion	kj
commencement	k/_	commune	kn
commend	k __	communicate	kuka
commendable	k __ b	communication	kukj
commendation	k __ ɟ	communion	knn
commensurable	k/ub	Communism	knȝ⌣
commensurate	k/ua	Communist	kn,
comment	k_	community	kn)
commentary	k_y	commutation	kuy
commentator	K_ a	commute	ku
commerce	krs	commuter	Ku
commercial	krx	compact	kpk
commiserate	ksa	compactness	kpk'
commiseration	ksy	companion	kpnn
commissariat	ksyl	company	co
commissary	ksy	comparable	kꝒb
commission	kj	comparative	kꝒv
commissioner	Kj	comparatively	kꝒvl
commit	kl	compare	kpa
committee	k)	comparison	kꝒsn
commodious	kdx	compartment	kp/_

compass	kp'	complexion	kpky
compassion	kpj	complexity	kpx)
compassionate	kpya	compliance	kpi√
compatible	kplb	compliant	kpi_
compatriot	kPal	complicate	kpka
compel	kpl	complication	kpkj
compensate	kp/a	complicity	kps)
compensation	kp/j	compliment	kp-
compete	kpe	complimentary	kp-y
competence	kpl√	comply	kpi
competency	kpl√	component	kpn-
competent	kpl-	comport	kp/
competition	kply	compose	kpʒ
competitive	kplv	composite	kpzl
competitor	Kpl	composition	kpzj
compilation	kplj	composure	kpʒ
compile	kpl	compound	kp——
complaisance	kps√	comprehend	kph——
complacent	kps-	comprehensible	kph√b
complain	kpn	comprehension	kphy
complainant	kpn-\	comprehensive	kph√v
complaint	kpa-	compress	kp'
complement	kp-	compression	kpj
complementary	kp-y	comprise	kpʒ
complete	kpe	compromise	kpↄ
completeness	kpe'	compulsion	kplj
completion	kpej	compulsory	kplsy
complex	kpx	compulsorily	kplsyl

46

compunction	kpqj	conclude	kcd
computation	kpuj	conclusion	kcj
compute	kpu	conclusive	kcsv
computer	Kpu	concoct	kkk
comrade	krd	concoction	kkkj
comradeship	krdʒ	concord	kk/
con	k	concordance	kk//
concave	kka	concordant	kk/-
conceal	ksl	concourse	kkrs
concealment	ksl-	concrete	kke
concede	ksd	concretion	kkj
conceit	kse	concubine	kkbn
conceivable	kseb	concupiscence	kkps/
conceive	kse	concur	kkr
concentrate	ks-a	concurrence	kkr/
concentration	ks-j	concussion	kkj
concentric	ks-k	condemn	kd
concept	ksp	condemnation	kdrj
conception	kspj	condensation	kd/j
concern	ksn	condense	kd/
concerning	ksn	condescend	kds-
concert	ks/	condign	kdn
concession	ksj	condiment	kd-
conciliate	ksla	condition	kdj
conciliation	kslj	conditional	kdjl
conciliatory	kslly	condole	kdl
concise	kss	condolence	kdl/
conclave	kcv	condonation	kdnj

47

condone	*kdn*	confirmative	*kfrv*
conduce	*kds*	confiscate	*kfska*
conducive	*kdsv*	conflagration	*kflgs*
conduct	*kdk*	conflict	*kflk*
conduction	*kdky*	conform	*kf*
conductor	*Kdk*	conformation	*kfy*
conduit	*kdl*	conformity	*kf)*
cone	*kn*	confound	*kf —*
confection	*kfky*	confront	*kf-*
confectioner	*Kfky*	confuse	*kf3*
confectionery	*kfkyy*	confusion	*kfy*
confederacy	*kJds,*	confutation	*kfuj*
confederate	*kJda*	confute	*kfu*
confederation	*kJdy*	congeal	*kyl*
confer	*kf*	congenial	*kynl*
conference	*kf*	congenital	*kynll*
confess	*kf '*	congest	*ky,*
confession	*kfy*	congestion	*kysy*
confessor	*Kf '*	conglomerate	*kglra*
confide	*kfd*	conglomeration	*kgly*
✓ confidence	*kfd*	congratulate	*kglla*
✓ confident	*kfd —*	congratulation	*kgly*
confidential	*kfdx*	congratulatory	*kgllay*
configuration	*kfgy*	congregate	*kgga*
confine	*kfi*	congregation	*kggy*
confinement	*kfi —*	congress	*kg '*
confirm	*kfrn*	congressional	*kgyl*
confirmation	*kfry*	congruent	*kgu —*

48

Word	Shorthand	Word	Shorthand
congruity	kgu)	consecrate	kska
conjecture	kjku	consecration	ksky
conjoin	kyyn	consecutive	kskv
conjugal	kygl	consent	ks-
conjugation	kygy	consequence	ksq/
conjunction	kyqy	consequent	ksq-
conjuncture	kyqu	consequential	ksqx
conjure	kyu	conservative	ksvv
connect	knk	conservatory	ksvly
connection	knky	conserve	ksv
connective	knkv	conserving	ksv
connects	knks	consider	Ks
connivance	ku/	considerable	Ksb
connive	ku	considerably	Ksb
connotation	knly	considerate	Ksa
connote	knl	consideration	Ksy
conquer	Kq	consign	ksin
conqueror	Kqr	consignment	ksin-
conquest	kq,,	consist	ks,
consanguinity	ksgn)	consistent	kss-
conscience	kZ/	consolation	ksly
conscientious	kZnx	console	ksl
conscientiously	kZnxl	consolidate	kslda
conscientiousness	kZnx'	consolidation	ksldy
conscious	kx	consonant	ksn-
consciousness	kx'	consort	ks/
conscript	kskp	conspicuous	kskx
conscription	kskpy	conspiracy	kss,

Word	Shorthand	Word	Shorthand
conspirator	*Ksl*	contagion	*klyn*
conspire	*ksu*	contagious	*klyx*
constable	*ksb*	contain	*kln*
constancy	*ks/*	container	*Kln*
constant	*ks-*	contaminate	*klrna*
constellation	*ksly*	contamination	*klry*
consternation	*kSry*	contemplate	*klpa*
constipate	*kspa*	contemplation	*klpy*
constituency	*kslw/*	contemporaneous	*klpnx*
constitute	*kslu*	contemporary	*klpy*
constitution	*ksly*	contempt	*kl*
constitutional	*kslyl*	contemptible	*klb*
constrain	*kSn*	contemptuous	*klx*
constraint	*kS-*	contend	*kl —*
constrict	*kSk*	content	*kl -*
constriction	*kSky*	contentedly	*kl=l*
construct	*kSk*	contention	*kly*
construction	*kSky*	contentment	*kl - -*
constructive	*kSkv*	contest	*kl,*
construe	*kSu*	context	*klx*
consul	*ksl*	contiguity	*klq)*
consular	*Ksl*	contiguous	*klgx*
consult	*ksll*	continent	*K-*
consultation	*kslly*	continental	*K-l*
consume	*ksu*	contingent	*Ky-*
consumer	*Ksu*	continual	*Kul*
consumption	*ksry*	continuance	*Kw/*
contact	*klk*	continuation	*Kuy*

50

Word	Outline	Word	Outline
continue	Ku	convalescent	kvls-
continuous	Kux	convene	kvn
contort	kl/	convenience	kv
contour	klu	convenient	kvn-
contraband	Kb—	convent	kv-
contract	Kk	convention	kvj
contraction	Kkj	conventionality	kvjl)
contractor	Kbr	converge	kvry
contradict	Kdk	convergence	kvry/
contradiction	Kdkj	conversant	kvrs-
contrary	Ky	conversation	kvrsj
contrast	K,	converse	kvrs
contravene	Kvn	convert	kv/
contravention	Kvj	convertible	kv/b
contribute	Kbu	convex	kvx
contributed	Kbū	convey	kva
contribution	Kbj	conveyance	kva/
contrite	Kl	convict	kvk
contrition	Kj	conviction	kvkj
contrivance	Kv/	convince	kv
contrive	Kv	convivial	kvvl
control	Kl	convocation	kvkj
controversy	Kvrs,	convoke	kvk
controvert	Kv/	convoy	kvy
contumacious	klrx	convulse	kvls
contumely	klrl	convulsion	kvlj
contusion	klj	convulsive	kvlsv
conundrum	k—⌢	cook	kk

✓ cooker	Kk	cordiality	k/l)
✓ cool	kul	cordon	k/n
cooler	Kl	corduroy	k/uy
coolness	kl'	core	ko
coop	kup	cork	kk
co-operate	kopa	cormorant	kvr-
co-operation	kopy	corn	kn
co-operative	kopv	cornea	kna
co-ordinate	k/na	corner	Kn
co-ordination	k/ny	cornet	knl
co-ordinative	k/rv	Cornish	knʒ
co-ordinator	K/na	cornucopia	knkpa
coot	ku	corollary	kly
cope	kop	corona	kna
coping	kop	coronation	kry
copious	kpx	coroner	Kn
copper	Kp	coronet	knl
copse	kps	corporal	kpl
copula	kpla	corporate	kpa
copulative	kplv	corporation	kpy
copy	kp,	corps	ko
copyright	kpru	corpse	kps
coquetry	kkl,	corpulence	kpl/
coquette	kkl	corpulent	kpl-
coracle	kK	corral	kl
coral	kl	correct	knk
cord	k/	correction	knky
cordial	k/l	corrective	knkv

52

Word	Shorthand	Word	Shorthand
correctly	*(shorthand)*	cost	*(shorthand)*
correctness	*(shorthand)*	costal	*(shorthand)*
corrector	*(shorthand)*	costive	*(shorthand)*
correlate	*(shorthand)*	costly	*(shorthand)*
correlation	*(shorthand)*	costume	*(shorthand)*
correspond	*(shorthand)*	cosy	*(shorthand)*
correspondence	*(shorthand)*	cot	*(shorthand)*
correspondent	*(shorthand)*	coterie	*(shorthand)*
corridor	*(shorthand)*	cottage	*(shorthand)*
corrigible	*(shorthand)*	cotton	*(shorthand)*
corroborate	*(shorthand)*	couch	*(shorthand)*
corroboration	*(shorthand)*	cough	*(shorthand)*
corroborative	*(shorthand)*	could	*(shorthand)*
corroboratory	*(shorthand)*	couldn't	*(shorthand)*
corrode	*(shorthand)*	council	*(shorthand)*
corrosion	*(shorthand)*	councillor	*(shorthand)*
corrosive	*(shorthand)*	counsel	*(shorthand)*
corrugate	*(shorthand)*	counsellor	*(shorthand)*
corrupt	*(shorthand)*	count	*(shorthand)*
corruptible	*(shorthand)*	countenance	*(shorthand)*
corruption	*(shorthand)*	counter	*(shorthand)*
corset	*(shorthand)*	counterbalance	*(shorthand)*
cortege	*(shorthand)*	counterfeit	*(shorthand)*
cortex	*(shorthand)*	countermand	*(shorthand)*
coruscate	*(shorthand)*	countersign	*(shorthand)*
corvette	*(shorthand)*	counterstroke	*(shorthand)*
cosmetic	*(shorthand)*	countess	*(shorthand)*
cosmopolitan	*(shorthand)*	countless	*(shorthand)*

Word	Shorthand	Word	Shorthand
country	K	cowl	k l
county	kl,	cowslip	k slp
coup	ku	coy	ky
couple	kp	cozy	kz,
couplet	kpl	crab	kb
coupling	kp	crack	kk
coupon	kpn	cracker	Kk
courage	ky	crackle	kK
courageous	kyx	cradle	kdl
course	kvs	craft	kf
court (ct)	k/	craftsman	kfsn -
courteous	k/x	crafty	kf,
courtesy 體貌	k/s,	crag	kq
courtier	K/e	cram	kn
court-martial	k/vrx	cramp	knp
courtship	k/3	cranberry	knby
cousin	kzn	crane	kn
cove	ko	craniology	knol
covenant	kvn -	cranium	kn
cover	Kv	crank	kq
covert	kv/	cranny	kn,
covet	kvl	crash	kʒ
covetous	kvlx	crass	k'
covey	kv,	crate	ka
cow	k	crater	Ka
coward	k/	cravat	kvl
cowardice	k/s	crave	ka
cowboy	k by	craven	kvn

54

English	Shorthand	English	Shorthand
crawl		crescendo	
crayon		crescent	
craze		cress	
crazy		crest	
creak		crestfallen	
cream		cretaceous	
creamery		cretonne	
creamy		crevasse	
crease		crevice	
create		crew	
creation		crewel	
creative		crib	
creator		cribbage	
creature		cricket	
credence		crier	
credential		crime	
credible		criminal	
credit		criminate	
creditable		criminology	
creditor		crimp	
credulity		crimson	
credulous		cringe	
creed		crinkle	
creek		crinoline	
creep		cripple	
cremation		crisis	
crepe		crisp	
crept		criterion	

critic	$k\sqrt{}$	crudity	$kd)$
critical	klK	cruel	kul
criticize	klz	cruelty	$kll,$
criticism	klz	cruet	kul
croak	kok	cruise	kz
crochet	kza	crumb	k
crock	kk	crumble	klb
crockery	kky	crumple	kp
crocodile	$kkdl$	crupper	Kp
crocus	kkx	crusade	ksd
croft	kf	crush	kz
crook	kk	crust	$k,$
crooked	$k\bar{k}$	crutch	kc
crop	kp	cry	ku
cross	k'	crypt	kp
crosswise	ks_3	crystal	ksl
crouch	kc	crystalline	ksl
croup	kup	crystallize	$kslz$
croupier	Kp	cub	kb
crow	ko	cube	kub
crowbar	$koba$	cubical	kbK
crowd	kd	cubist	$kb,$
crown	kn	cuckoo	kku
crucial	kx	cucumber	Kkb
crucible	ksb	cuddle	kdl
crucifixion	$ksfk$	cudgel	kjl
crucify	ksf	cue	ku
crude	kd	cuff	kf

cuisine	*kzn*	curious	*kyx*
culinary	*klny*	curl	*krl*
cull	*kl*	curlew	*krlu*
culminate	*klna*	curly	*krl*
culmination	*klny*	currant	*kr-*
culpable	*klpb*	currency	*kr/*
culprit	*klpl*	current	*kr-*
cultivate	*kllva*	curry	*ky*
cultivation	*klly*	curse	*krs*
culture	*kllu*	cursory	*krsy*
cumber	*Kb*	curtail	*k/l*
cumbersome	*Kbs*	curtain	*k/n*
cumbrous	*kbx*	curtsy	*k/s,*
cumulate	*kla*	curvature	*krvlu*
cumulation	*kl*	curve	*krv*
cunning	*knq*	cushion	*ky*
cup	*kp*	custard	*kSd*
cupboard	*kb/*	custodian	*ksdn*
cupidity	*kpd)*	custody	*ksd,*
cupola	*kpla*	custom	*ks*
cur	*kr*	customary	*ksry*
curate	*kua*	customer	*Ks*
curator	*Kua*	cut	*kl*
curb	*krb*	cute	*ku*
curd	*k/*	cuticle	*klK*
cure	*ku*	cutlery	*klly*
curfew	*krfu*	cutlet	*klll*
curiosity	*kys)*	cutter	*Kl*

cuttlefish	*kłłfʒ*	cynic	*snk*
cycle	*sk*	cynical	*snk*
cyclone	*skln*	cynicism	*snsz*
cylinder	*sl—*	cypress	*sp'*
cylindrical	*sl—K*	czar	*za*
cymbal	*smb*		

D

dab	*db*	damnation	*dny*
dad	*dd*	damp	*dp*
daddy	*dd,*	dampness	*dp'*
dado	*ddo*	damper	*Dp*
daffodil	*dfdl*	damsel	*dzl*
dagger	*Dg*	damson	*dzn*
daily	*dl*	dance	*d/*
daintiness	*d-'*	dancer	*D/*
dainty	*d-,*	dandelion	*d—ln*
dairy	*dy*	dandruff	*d—f*
daisy	*dz,*	dandy	*d—,*
dale	*dal*	danger	*Dɟ*
dally	*dl,*	dangerous	*Dɟx*
dam	*dn*	dangle	*dgl*
damage	*dy*	dank	*dq,*
damageable	*dyb*	dapper	*Dp*
damask	*dsk*	dapple	*dp*
dame	*da*	dare	*da*
damn	*dn*	daring	*da*
damnable	*dnb*	dark	*drk*

58

Word	Shorthand	Word	Shorthand
darken	drkn	deadly	ddl
darker	Drk	deaf	df
darkly	drkl	deafen	dfn
darkness	drk'	deafness	df'
darling	drlg	deal	dl
darn	drn	dealer	Dl
dart	d/	dealing	dl
dash	dʒ	dealings	dl
dastard	dʃd	dean	dn
data	dla	deanery	dny
date	da	dear	de
daub	dab	dearer	De
daughter	Da	dearly	del
daunt	da-	dearth	drl
dauntless	d-l'	death	dl
davit	dvl	deathbed	dlbd
dawdle	ddl	deathless	dll'
dawn	dan	debar	dba
day	d	debase	dbs
daybreak	dbk	debatable	dbab
daylight	dli	debate	dba
daytime	dli	debauchery	dbcy
daze	dʒ	debenture	db-u
dazzle	dzl	debilitate	dblla
deacon	dkn	debit	dbl
dead	dd	debouch	dbʒ
deaden	ddn	debris	dbe
deadliness	ddl'	debt	dl

59

Word	Shorthand	Word	Shorthand
debtor	Dl	declamatory	dc~ly
decade	dkd	declarable	dcb
decadence	dkd/	declaration	dcy
decamp	dk~p	declarative	dcv
decant	dk-	declare	dc
decanter	Dk-	declension	dcy
decapitate	dkpla	decline	dcn
decay	dka	decliner	Dcn
decease	dss	declinometer	dcnle
deceit	dse	declivity	dcv)
deceitful	dsef	decoction	dkky
deceive	dse	decompose	dkp3
deceiver	Dse	decomposition	dkpzy
December	dc	decorate	dka
decent	ds-	decoration	dky
decency	ds/	decorative	dkv
deception	dspy	decorator	Dka
deceptive	dspv	decorous	dkx
decide	dsd	decorum	dk~
decidedly	dsd	decoy	dky
deciduous	dsdx	decrease	dks
decimal (dec)	dsl	decree	dke
decipher	dsf	decrement	dk-
decison	dsy	decrepit	dkpl
decisive	dsuv	decrepitude	dkpld
deck	dk	decry	dke
declaim	dc~	dedicate	dolka
declamation	dc~y	dedication	ddky

deduce		defence	
deduct		defenceless	
deductable		defencible	
deed		defensive	
deem		defer	
deep		deference	
deepen		deferential	
deeper		defiance	
deeply		defiant	
deepness		deficiency	
deer		deficient	
deface		deficit	
defacement		defile	
defalcate		definable	
defalcation		define	
defamation		definite	
defamatory		definition	
defame		definitive	
default		deflect	
defeasible		deflower	
defeat		deform	
defect		deformity	
defection		defraud	
defective		defray	
defence		deft	
defend		defunct	
defendant		defy	
defender		degenerate	

61

Word	Shorthand	Word	Shorthand
degeneration		delinquency	
degradation		delinquent	
degrade		delirious	
degree		delirium	
deification		deliver	
deify		deliverance	
deign		deliverer	
deity		delivery	
dejected		dell	
dejection		delta	
delay		delude	
delectable		deluge	
delegate		delusion	
delegation		delusive	
delete		delve	
deleterious		demagogue	
deletion		demand	
deliberate		demarcation	
deliberation		demean	
deliberative		demeanour	
delicacy		demise	
delicate		demobilization	
delicious		demobilize	
delight		democracy	
delightful		democrat	
delineate		democratic	
delineation		demolish	
delineator		demolition	

62

Word	Outline	Word	Outline
demon		dental	
demoniac		dentist	
demoniacal		dentistry	
demonstrable		denudation	
demonstrate		denude	
demonstration		denunciate	
demonstrative		denunciation	
demoralization		deny	
demoralize		depart	
demur		department (dpt)	
demure		departure	
demureness		depend	
demurring		dependence	
den		dependency	
denial		dependent	
denizen		depict	
denominate		deplete	
denomination		depletion	
denominator		deplorable	
denotation		deplore	
denote		deploy	
denouement		deponent	
denounce		depopulate	
denouncement		depopulation	
dense		deport	
denseness		deportation	
density		deportment	
dent		depose	

deposit	dpzl	derisory	drsy
depository	dpzly	derivation	dry
depositor	Dpzl	derivative	druv
depot	dpo	derive	dru
depravation	dpvy	derogate	drga
deprave	dpa	derogatory	drgly
depravity	dpv)	derrick	drk
deprecate	dpka	descant	dsk -
deprecatory	dpkay	descend	ds ——
depreciate	dpʒa	descendant	ds —— -
depreciation	dpʒy	descent	ds -
depreciatory	dpʒay	describe	des
depredation	dpdy	description	des
depress	dp'	descriptive	desv
depression	dpy	desecrate	dska
deprivation	dpvy	desecration	dsky
deprive	dpu	desert	dʒ/
depth	dpl	desertion	dry
deputation	dply	deserve	dsv
depute	dpu	desiccate	dska
deputize	dplʒ	desiderate	Dsa
deputy	dpl,	desideratum	Dsa
derange	dry	design	dʒın
derangement	dry -	designate	dʒgra
derelict	drlk	designation	dʒgry
deride	drd	designer	Dʒın
derision	dry	desirable	dʒıb
derisive	drsv	desire	dʒı

64

Word	Outline	Word	Outline
desirous	dzıx	destructive	dℓkv
desist	ds,	desultory	dlℓy
desk	drk	detach	dℓc
desolate	drla	detachment	dℓc-
desolation	drly	detail	dℓℓ
despair	dsa	detain	dℓn
despatch	dec	detect	dℓk
desperate	dsa	detection	dℓky
desperation	dsy	detective	dℓkv
despicable	dskb	detector	Dℓk
despise	dez	detention	dy
despite	dsı 不管…	deter	D
despoil	dsyl	detergent	Dy-
despoliation	dsly	deteriorate	Dra
despondency	ds—⟋	deterioration	Dry
despondent	ds—-	determinate	Drna
despot	del	determination	Dry
despotism	delzn	determine	Drn
dessert	dз/	determined	Drn̄
destination	dsry	deterrent	D-
destine	dsn	detest	dℓ,
destiny	dsn,	detestable	dℓsb
destitute	drlu	detestation	dℓsy
destitution	drly	dethrone	dℓn
destroy	dЅy	detonate	dℓna
destroyer	DЅy	detour	dℓu
destructible	dskb	detract	Dk
destruction	dsky	detriment	D-

65

detrimental	D-l	dialect	dlk
deuce	dus	dialectic	dlkT
devastate	dvsa	dialogue	dlg
devastation	dvy	diameter	dre
develop	dvlp	diametrically	drek
development	dvlp-	diamond	dn—
deviate	dva	diaper	Dp
device	dvs	diaphanous	dfnx
devil	dvl	diaphragm	df
devious	dvx	diarrhoea	Di˝
devise	dvz	diary	dy
devoid	dvyd	diatonic	dlnk
devolution	dvly	diatribe	dlb
devolve	dvlv	dice	dus
devote	dvo	dictate	dka
devotion	dvy	dictation	dkly
devour	Dv	dictator	Dka
devout	dvl	dictatorial	dklyl
dew	du	diction	dky
dewdrop	dudp	dictionary	dkyy
dexterity	Dx)	dictum	dk
dexterous	Dx	did	dd
diabolic	dblk	didn't	dd-
diadem	dd	die	du
diagnosis	dgnss	diesel	dzl
diagonal	dgnl	diet	dul
diagram	dg	differ	df
dial	dul	difference	df

66

different	*dp-*	diligent	*dly-*
difficult	*dfk*	dilute	*dlu*
difficulties	*dfks*	dilution	*dly*
difficulty	*dfk*	dim	*dn*
diffident	*dfd-*	dime	*du*
diffuse	*dfs* *diffused 18.9.m*	dimension	*dry*
diffusive	*dfsv*	diminish	*drnʒ*
dig	*dq*	diminution	*drny*
digest	*dy,*	diminutive	*drnv*
digestible	*dysb*	dimple	*drp*
digestion	*dyry*	din	*dn*
digestive	*dysv*	dine	*dun*
digger	*Dq*	dinghy	*dq,*
dignify	*dgnf*	dingy	*dy,*
dignitary	*dgnly*	dinner	*Dn*
dignity	*dgn)*	diocese	*dss*
digress	*dq'*	dip	*dp*
digression	*dgy*	diptheria	*dflya*
dike	*duk*	diphthong	*dflq*
dilapidated	*dlpdā*	diploma	*dpra*
dilapidation	*dlpdy*	diplomacy	*dprs,*
dilatable	*dlab*	diplomat	*dprl*
dilatation	*dlly*	diplomatic	*dprJ*
dilate	*dla*	diplomatist	*dprl,*
dilatory	*dlly*	dipsomania	*dprna*
dilemma	*dlra*	dire	*du*
dilettante	*dll-,*	direct	*drk*
diligence	*dly/*	direction	*drky*

directive	*drkv*	disastrous	*dzsx*
directly	*drkl*	disband	*dsb —*
director	*Drk*	disbelief	*dsblf*
dirge	*drj*	disburse	*dsbrs*
dirigible	*dryb*	disc	*dsk*
dirt	*d/*	discard	*dsk/*
dirty	*d/,*	discern	*dsn*
disable	*dsb*	discernible	*dsnb*
disabuse	*dsbz*	discerning	*dsn‾*
disadvantage	*dsavy*	discernment	*dsn -*
disaffection	*dsfky*	discharge	*dscq*
disagree	*dsAq*	disciple	*dsp*
disagreeable	*dsAqb*	disciplinarian	*dspnyn*
disagreement	*dsAq-*	disciplinary	*dspry*
disallow	*dsl*	discipline	*dspn*
disappear	*dsap*	disclaim	*dskla*
disappearance	*dsap/*	disclose	*dsklz*
disappoint	*dspy-*	disclosure	*dsklz/*
disappointment	*dspy--*	discoloration	*dsKly*
disapprobation	*dspbj*	discolour	*dsKl*
disapprove	*dspv*	discomfit	*dskfl*
disarm	*dsa*	discomfiture	*dskflu*
disarmament	*dsa -*	discompose	*dskpz*
disarrange	*dsry*	discomposure	*dskpz/*
disarray	*dsra*	disconcert	*dsks/*
disassociate	*dssZa*	disconnect	*dsknk*
disassociation	*dssZj*	disconnection	*dsknkj*
disaster	*dzS*	disconsolate	*dsksla*

68

discontent		disdainful	
discontentment		disease	
discontinuation		disembark	
discontinue		disembody	
discontinuous		disenchant	
discord		disenchantment	
discordant		disendow	
discount		disengage	
discourage		disentangle	
discouragement		disestablish	
discourse		disfavour	
discourteous		disfigure	
discover		disfigurement	
discoverer		disgorge	
discovery		disgrace	
discredit		disgraceful	
discreditable		disguise	
discreet		disgust	
discrepancy		dish	
discretion		dishearten	
discretionary		dishevel	
discriminate		dishonest	
discrimination		dishonesty	
discriminative		dishonour	
discursive		dishonourable	
discuss		disillusion	
discussion		disillusionment	
disdain		disincline	

69

Word	Shorthand	Word	Shorthand
disinfect		disown	
disinfectant		disparage	
disingenuous		disparagement	
disinherit		disparity	
disintegrate		dispassionate	
disintegration		dispatch	
disinterested		dispel	
disjoint		dispensable	
disc		dispensary	
dislike		dispensation	
dislocate		dispense	
dislocation		disperse	
dislodge		dispersion	
disloyal		dispirit	
disloyalty		displace	
dismal		display	
dismantle		displease	
dismay		displeasure	
dismember		disposal	
dismiss		dispose	
dismissal		disposition	
dismount		dispossess	
disobedience		disproportionate	
disobedient		disprove	
disobey		disputation	
disorder		dispute	
disorganization		disqualification	
disorganize		disqualify	

Word	Shorthand	Word	Shorthand
disquiet	*dsql*	dissociate	*dsʒa*
disregard	*dsrq/*	dissoluble	*dslb*
disrepair	*dsrpa*	dissolute	*dslu*
disreputable	*dsrpub*	dissolution	*dsly*
disrepute	*dsrpu*	dissolve	*dzlv*
disrespect	*dsrsk*	dissonant	*dsn-*
disrespectful	*dsrslf*	dissuade	*ds-d*
disrobe	*dsrb*	distaff	*dsf*
disruption	*dsrpy*	distance	*ds/*
disruptive	*dsrpv*	distant	*ds-*
dissatisfaction	*dsal*	distaste	*ds,*
dissatisfied	*dsaī*	distasteful	*dssf*
dissatisfy	*dsal*	distemper	*dsĪp*
dissect	*dsk*	distend	*ds—*
dissemble	*dsrb*	distil	*dsl*
dissembler	*Dsrb*	distillation	*dsly*
disseminate	*dsrna*	distiller	*Dsl*
dissemination	*dsry*	distillery	*dsly*
dissension	*dsy*	distinct	*dsq*
dissent	*ds-*	distinction	*dsqy*
dissertation	*ds/|*	distinctive	*dsqv*
disservice	*dsvs*	distinguish	*dsqß*
dissimilar	*dsrl*	distinguished	*dsqß̃*
dissimilarity	*dsrl)*	distort	*dsl*
dissimilitude	*dsrlld*	distortion	*dsy*
dissimulation	*dsrly*	distract	*dsk*
dissipate	*dspa*	distraction	*dsky*
dissipation	*dspy*	distraught	*dsl*

Word	Outline	Word	Outline
distress		dividends	
distressful		dividing	
distribute		divination	
distribution		divine	
distributive		divinity	
district		divisibility	
distrust		divisible	
distrustful		division	
disturb		divisor	
disturbance		divorce	
disuse		divulge	
ditch		dizzy	
ditto		do	
ditty		docile	
diurnal		dock	
divan		docket	
divaricate		doctor	
dive		doctrinaire	
diver		doctrine	
diverge		document	
divergent		documentary	
diverse		dodge	
diversity		doe	
divert		does	
divest		doesn't	
divestment		doff	
divide		dog	
dividend		doggerel	

dogma	*dgra*	done	*dn*
dogmatic	*dgr*	donkey	*dq,*
dogmatism	*dgrlz*	donor	*Dn*
dogmatize	*dgrlz*	don't	*do-*
doily	*dyl*	doom	*du*
doings	*du*	door	*do*
doldrums	*dldrs*	doorstep	*dosp*
doleful	*dlf*	doorway	*dowa*
doll	*dl*	dormant	*dr -*
dollar	*Dl*	dormitory	*drrly*
dolly	*dl,*	dorsal	*drsl*
dolorous	*Dlx*	dose	*dos*
dolphin	*dlfn*	dot	*dl*
dolt	*doll*	dotage	*doq*
domain	*drn*	dotard	*do/*
dome	*do*	dote	*do*
domestic	*dS*	double	*db*
domesticate	*drska*	doubt	*dl*
domicile	*drsl*	doubtful	*dlf*
dominant	*drn -*	doubtless	*dll'*
dominate	*drna*	douche	*duß*
domination	*drry*	dough	*do*
domineer	*drne*	doughnut	*donl*
dominical	*drnK*	doughty	*dl,*
dominion	*drrn*	dove	*dv*
domino	*drno*	dowdy	*dd,*
don	*dn*	dower	*D*
donation	*dry*	down	*dn*

73

Word	Outline	Word	Outline
downcast	*(shorthand)*	drawbridge	*(shorthand)*
downright	*(shorthand)*	drawer	*(shorthand)*
downstairs	*(shorthand)*	drawl	*(shorthand)*
downward	*(shorthand)*	drawn	*(shorthand)*
downwards	*(shorthand)*	dray	*(shorthand)*
dowry	*(shorthand)*	dread	*(shorthand)*
doze	*(shorthand)*	dreadful	*(shorthand)*
dozen	*(shorthand)*	dream	*(shorthand)*
drab	*(shorthand)*	dreamer	*(shorthand)*
drachm	*(shorthand)*	dreary	*(shorthand)*
draft	*(shorthand)*	dreg	*(shorthand)*
drag	*(shorthand)*	drench	*(shorthand)*
dragon	*(shorthand)*	dress	*(shorthand)*
dragoon	*(shorthand)*	dresser	*(shorthand)*
drain	*(shorthand)*	dressmaker	*(shorthand)*
drainage	*(shorthand)*	drew	*(shorthand)*
drake	*(shorthand)*	dribble	*(shorthand)*
dram	*(shorthand)*	dried	*(shorthand)*
drama	*(shorthand)*	drier	*(shorthand)*
dramatic	*(shorthand)*	drift	*(shorthand)*
drank	*(shorthand)*	driftwood	*(shorthand)*
drape	*(shorthand)*	drill	*(shorthand)*
drapery	*(shorthand)*	drink	*(shorthand)*
drastic	*(shorthand)*	drinker	*(shorthand)*
draught	*(shorthand)*	drip	*(shorthand)*
draughtsman	*(shorthand)*	drive	*(shorthand)*
draw	*(shorthand)*	drivel	*(shorthand)*
drawback	*(shorthand)*	driver	*(shorthand)*

Word	Shorthand	Word	Shorthand
drizzle		dub	
droll		dubiety	
dromedary		dubious	
drone		duchess	
droop		duck	
drop		duckling	
dropsy		duct	
dross		ductile	
drought		dudgeon	
drove		due	
drown		duel	
drowsiness		duellist	
drowsy		duet	
drudge		dug	
drudgery		duke	
drug		dulcet	
drugget		dull	
druggist		dullness	
drum		duly	
drunk		dumb	
drunkard		dump	
drunken		dun	
drunkenness		dunce	
dry		dung	
dryad		dungeon	
dryer		duo	
dryly		dupe	
dual		duplicate	

75

duplication		dwarf	
duplicity		dwell	
durable		dwelling	
duration		dwelt	
duress		dwindle	
during		dye	
dusk		dying	
dusky		dynamic	
dust		dynamite	
duster		dynamo	
dusty		dynasty	
dutiable		dysentry	
dutifully		dyspepsia	
duty		dyspeptic	

E

each		earning	
eager		earth	
eagerness		earthen	
eagle		earthly	
ear		earthward	
earl		ease	
earldom		easel	
earlier		easier	
early		easily	
earn		east	
earnest		Easter	
earnestness		easterly	

Word	Shorthand	Word	Shorthand
eastern	Ern	edible	edb
eastward	E /	edict	edk
easy	ez	edification	edf
eat	el	edifice	edps
eatable	elb	edify	edp
eater	EL	edit	edl
eaves	evs	edition	edy
ebb	eb	editor	Edl
ebony	ebn,	editorial	edlyl
ebullient	ebl -	educate	edka
eccentric	x - k	education	edky
eccentricity	x - b)	educational	edkyl
ecclesiastic	eklzS	educe	eds
echo	eko	eel	el
eclat	ekla	eerie	E,
eclectic	eklkT	efface	efs
eclipse	eklps	effacement	efs -
ecology	ekol	effect	efk
economic	eknk	effective	efkv
economical	eknK	effectual	efkl
economist	ekn,	effeminacy	efrns,
economy	ekn,	effeminate	efrna
ecstasy	xls,	effervesce	efvs
ecstatic	xlT	effervescence	efvs'
eczema	xna	effervescent	efvs -
eddy	ad,	effete	efe
edge	ej	efficacious	efkx
edging	ej	efficiency	efZ

77

D.—F

Word	Outline	Word	Outline
efficient	*ef3-*	elaborate	*e Lba*
effort	*ep/*	elaborately	*eLbal*
effrontery	*ef-y*	elaboration	*eLby*
effulgent	*efly-*	elapse	*elps*
effusion	*eff*	elastic	*elS*
effusive	*efsv*	elasticity	*elss)*
egg	*eq*	elate	*ela*
egoism	*egz*	elation	*ely*
egoist	*eq,*	elbow	*elbo*
egotist	*egl,*	elder	*El*
egotistical	*eglsk*	elderberry	*Elby*
egregious	*egsx*	eldest	*eld,*
egress	*eq'*	elect	*elk*
eider	*J*	election	*elky*
eiderdown	*Idun*	elector	*Elk*
eight	*8*	electric	*Elk*
eighteen	*18*	electrical	*ElK*
eighteenth	*18L*	electrically	*ElK*
eighth	*8L*	electrician	*Ely*
eighty	*80*	electricity	*Els)*
either	*E J*	electrifiable	*Elfb*
ejaculate	*ejkla*	electrification	*Elf*
ejaculation	*ejkly*	electrified	*Elf*
ejaculatory	*ejklay*	electrify	*Elf*
eject	*ejk*	electrifying	*Elf*
ejection	*ejky*	electro	*El*
ejectment	*ejk-*	electrocardiograph	*Elk/gl*
eke	*ek*	electrocardiogram	*Elk/g*

78

electrocute	*Elku*	eleventh	*11 L*
electrocution	*Elky*	elf	*elf*
electrode	*Eld*	elicit	*elsl*
electrolier	*Elle*	elide	*eld*
electrology	*Elol*	eligibility	*eljb)*
electrolysis	*Ellss*	eligible	*eljb*
electrolyte	*Elli*	eliminate	*elrna*
electrolyze	*Ellz*	elimination	*elrny*
electro-magnet	*Elrgl*	elision	*elj*
electro-magnetism	*Elrglz*	ellipse	*elps*
electrometer	*Elre*	elm	*elr*
electromotor	*Elro*	elocution	*elky*
electroplate	*Elpa*	elongate	*elga*
electroscope	*Elskp*	elope	*elp*
electrotype	*Ellp*	eloquence	*elg*
electrotyper	*El Ip*	eloquent	*elg-*
eleemosynary	*elrsny*	else	*ls*
elegance	*elg*	elsewhere	*lsur*
elegant	*elg-*	elucidate	*elsda*
elegy	*elj,*	elucidation	*elsdy*
element	*el-*	elude	*eld*
elementary	*el-y*	elusion	*elj*
elephant	*elf-*	elusive	*elsv*
elephantine	*elf-n*	elusory	*elsy*
elevate	*elva*	elves	*elvs*
elevation	*elvy*	elysium	*elzr*
elevator	*Elva*	emaciate	*erza*
eleven	*11*	emaciation	*erzl*

emanate		embrocation	
emanation		embroider	
emancipate		embroidery	
emancipation		embroil	
emasculate		embryo	
embalm		embryonic	
embankment		emend	
embargo		emendation	
embark		emerald	
embarkation		emerge	
embarrass		emergency	
embarrassment		emeritus	
embassy		emersion	
embellish		emery	
embellishment		emetic	
ember		emigrant	
embezzle		emigrate	
embitter		emigration	
emblazon		eminence	
emblazonry		eminent	
emblem		emission	
emblematic		emit	
embody		emollient	
embolden		emolument	
emboss		emotion	
embossment		emperor	
embrace		emphasize	
embrasure		emphatic	

Word	Outline	Word	Outline
empire		enclitic	
empiric		enclose	
empiricism		enclosure	
employ		encomium	
employee		encompass	
employer		encore	
employment		encounter	
emporium		encourage	
empress		encouragement	
emptiness		encroach	
empty		encroachment	
empyreal		encrust	
emulate		encumber	
emulation		encumbrance	
emulsion		encyclical	
enable		encyclopaedia	
enact		end	
enactment		endanger	
enamel		endear	
enamour		endearment	
encamp		endeavour	
encase		endemic	
encaustic		ending	
enchant		endless	
enchanter		endogen	
enchantment		endorse	
enchantress		endorsement	
encircle		endow	

Word	Shorthand	Word	Shorthand
endowment		enjoin	
endue		enjoy	
endurance		enjoyable	
endure		enjoyment	
enema		enlarge	
enemy		enlargement	
energetic		enlighten	
energy		enlightenment	
enervate		enlist	
enfeeble		enlistment	
enfold		enliven	
enforce		enmity	
enfranchise		enoble	
engage		ennui	
engagement		enormous	
engender		enough	
engine		enquire	
engineer		enrage	
England		enrapture	
English		enrich	
engrain		enrol	
engrave		enrolment	
engraver		ensconce	
engross		enshrine	
engulf		ensign	
enhance		enslave	
enigma		ensnare	
enigmatic		ensue	

ensure	ↄ̸ʒu	entree	ↄa
entablature	ↄlblu	entrench	ↄc
entail	ↄll	entrust	ↄ,
entangle	ↄlgl	entry	ↄ,
entanglement	ↄlgl-	entwine	ↄlↄn
enter	ↄ	enumerate	elↄa
enteric	ↄk	enumeration	elↄy
enterprise	ↄpʒ	enumerator	elↄar
enterprising	ↄpʒ	enunciate	ↄ√a
entertain	ↄln	enunciation	ↄ√₁
entertainment	ↄln-	envelop	ↄvlp
enthrall	ↄll	envelope	ↄvlp
enthrone	ↄln	envelopment	ↄvlp-
enthusiasm	ↄlzz	enviable	ↄvb
enthusiast	ↄlz,	envious	ↄvc
enthusiastic	ↄlzS	environ	ↄvↄn
entice	ↄls	environment	ↄvↄn-
entire	ↄlu	environs	ↄvↄns
entirely	ↄlul	envisage	ↄvzl
entitle	ↄttl	envoy	ↄvy
entity	ↄl)	envy	ↄv,
entomb	ↄlu	epaulet	epll
entomologist	ↄlↄol,	ephemeral	efↄl
entomology	ↄlↄol	epic	epk
entrails	ↄls	epicure	epku
entrance	ↄv	epicycle	epsK
entreat	ↄl	epidemic	epdↄk
entreaty	ↄl,	epidermis	Epↄs

83

epiglottis	*(shorthand)*	equidistant	*(shorthand)*
epigram	*(shorthand)*	equilateral	*(shorthand)*
epigraph	*(shorthand)*	equilibrium	*(shorthand)*
epilepsy	*(shorthand)*	equine	*(shorthand)*
epileptic	*(shorthand)*	equinoctial	*(shorthand)*
epilogue	*(shorthand)*	equinox	*(shorthand)*
episcopal	*(shorthand)*	equip	*(shorthand)*
episcopate	*(shorthand)*	equipage	*(shorthand)*
episode	*(shorthand)*	equivalent	*(shorthand)*
epistle	*(shorthand)*	equivocal	*(shorthand)*
epitaph	*(shorthand)*	equivocate	*(shorthand)*
epithet	*(shorthand)*	equivocation	*(shorthand)*
epitome	*(shorthand)*	era	*(shorthand)*
epitomize	*(shorthand)*	eradicate	*(shorthand)*
epoch	*(shorthand)*	erase	*(shorthand)*
equability	*(shorthand)*	eraser	*(shorthand)*
equable	*(shorthand)*	erect	*(shorthand)*
equal	*(shorthand)*	erection	*(shorthand)*
equality	*(shorthand)*	ermine	*(shorthand)*
equalization	*(shorthand)*	erode	*(shorthand)*
equanimity	*(shorthand)*	erosion	*(shorthand)*
equate	*(shorthand)*	erosive	*(shorthand)*
equation	*(shorthand)*	erotic	*(shorthand)*
equator	*(shorthand)*	err	*(shorthand)*
equatorial	*(shorthand)*	errand	*(shorthand)*
equerry	*(shorthand)*	errant	*(shorthand)*
equestrian	*(shorthand)*	errantry	*(shorthand)*
equiangular	*(shorthand)*	erratic	*(shorthand)*

84

erroneous	ɛɾɒ	establish	esl
error	ɛ	establishment	esl-
eructation	erkl	estate	esa
erudite	erdi	esteem	ese
erupt	erp	estimable	esrb
eruption	erpl	estimate	esra
eruptive	erpv	estimation	esrl
erysipelas	ersps	estrange	esl
escalade	eskld	estrangement	esl-
escalator	Eskl	estuary	esy
escapade	eskpd	et cetera	elc
escape	eskp	etch	ec
escarp	eskrp	eternal	Enl
eschew	escu	eternity	En)
escort	esk/	ether	E
esoteric	eslrk	ethereal	elyl
esparto	es/o	ethic	elk
especial	esx	ethical	elK
especially	esx	ethnic	elnk
espionage	esrl	ethnography	elngl,
esplanade	esrd	etiquette	elkl
espouse	es3	etymology	elrol
espy	esu	eucalyptus	uklpx
esquire	esq	eugenic	ynk
essay	esa	eulogist	ulj,
essayist	esa,	eulogize	ulj3
essence	es/	eulogy	ulj,
essential	esx	eunuch	unk

euphemism		everywhere	
euphony		evict	
Europe		evidence	
euthanasia		evident	
evacuate		evil	
evade		evildoer	
evaluate		evince	
evaluation		eviscerate	
evaporate		evoke	
evasion		evolution	
evasive		evolve	
eve		ewe	
even		ewer	
evening		exacerbate	
evenly		exacerbation	
evenness		exact	
event		exactitude	
eventide		exactly	
eventual		exactness	
ever		exactor	
evergreen		exaggerate	
everlasting		exaggeration	
evermore		exalt	
every		exaltation	
everybody		examination	
everyday		examine	
everyone		examiner	
everything		example	

86

exasperate	*xea*	excoriate	*xka*
exasperation	*xey*	excrement	*xk-*
excavate	*xkva*	excrescence	*xks/*
excavation	*xkvy*	excrete	*xke*
exceed	*xd*	excruciate	*xkʒa*
exceeding	*xd*	exculpate	*xklpa*
exceedingly	*xdl*	excursion	*xkry*
excel	*xl*	excusable	*xkzb*
excellence	*xl/*	excuse	*xkʒ (v) xks (n)*
excellency	*xl/*	execrable	*xkb*
excellent	*xl-*	execrate	*xka*
except	*xp*	execration	*xky*
exception	*xpy*	execute	*xku*
exceptional	*xpyl*	execution	*xky*
excerpt	*xrp*	executioner	*Xky*
excess	*x'*	executive	*xkv*
excessive	*xsv*	executor	*Xku*
exchange	*xcy*	executrix	*xklx*
exchequer	*Xck*	exegesis	*xpss*
excise	*x3*	exemplar	*Xrp*
excite	*xu*	exemplary	*xrpy*
excitement	*xu-*	exemplification	*xrpf*
exclaim	*xc⌒*	exempt	*x⌒*
exclamation	*xc⌒y*	exemption	*x⌒y*
exclamatory	*xc⌒ly*	exercise	*Xsʒ*
exclude	*xcd*	exert	*x/*
exclusive	*xcsv*	exertion	*Xy*
excommunicate	*xkuka*	exhalation	*xhly*

Word	Outline	Word	Outline
exhale	*xhl*	expansive	*xp/v*
exhaust	*x,*	expatiate	*xpʒa*
exhaustion	*xsy*	expatriate	*xPaa*
exhaustive	*xsv*	expect	*xpk*
exhibit	*xbl*	expectancy	*xpk/*
exhibition	*xby*	expectant	*xpk-*
exhibitor	*Xbl*	expectation	*xpky*
exhilarate	*Xla*	expectorate	*Xpka*
exhilaration	*Xly*	expedient	*xpd-*
exhort	*x/*	expedite	*xpdu*
exhortation	*x/ₗ*	expedition	*xpdy*
exhume	*xu*	expel	*xpl*
exigency	*xy/*	expend	*xp —*
exigent	*xy-*	expenditure	*xp —lu*
exile	*xl*	expense	*xp/*
exist	*x,*	expensive	*xp/v*
existed	*xš*	experience	*xP*
existence	*xs/*	experiment	*xP-*
exit	*xl*	expert	*xp/*
exodus	*xdx*	expiable	*xpb*
exonerate	*xOna*	expiate	*xpa*
exorbitant	*xobl-*	expiration	*xpiy*
exorcize	*Xsz*	expire	*xpu*
exoteric	*xbrk*	explain	*xpn*
exotic	*xᴛ*	explanation	*xpny*
expand	*xp —*	expletive	*xpv*
expanse	*xp/*	explicate	*xpka*
expansion	*xpy*	explicit	*xpsl*

88

explode	*xpd*	extendable	*xl —b*
exploit	*xpyl*	extension	*xly*
exploitation	*xpyly*	extensive	*xl/v*
exploration	*xpoy*	extent	*xl-*
exploratory	*xprly*	extenuate	*xlna*
explore	*xpo*	exterior	*Xr*
explorer	*Xpo*	exterminate	*Xrna*
explosion	*xpy*	extermination	*Xrny*
exponent	*xpn-*	external	*Xrl*
export	*xp/*	extinct	*xlq*
expose	*xp3*	extinction	*xlqy*
exposition	*xp3y*	extinguish	*xlqß*
expostulate	*xpsla*	extinguisher	*Xlqß*
exposure	*xpz/*	extirpate	*Xpa*
expound	*xp —*	extol	*xll*
express	*xp'*	extort	*xl/*
expression	*xpy*	extortion	*xbry*
expressive	*xpsv*	extortionate	*xbrya*
expressly	*xpsl*	extra	*X*
expulsion	*xply*	extract	*Xk*
expunge	*xpy*	extraction	*Xky*
expurgate	*xpga*	extradite	*Xde*
exquisite	*xqzl*	extradition	*Xdy*
extant	*xl-*	extraneous	*Xrx*
extemporaneous	*xl prx*	extraordinary	*Xodny*
extempore	*xl po*	extravagance	*Xvq/*
extemporize	*xl p3*	extravagant	*Xvq-*
extend	*xl —*	extreme	*X*

extremity	$X\frown)$	exultant	$xll-$
extricable	Xkb	exultation	xll
extricate	Xka	eye	$\smile$
extrovert	$Xv/$	eyeball	bl
exuberance	Xb	eyebrow	$b\frown$
exuberant	$Xb-$	eyelet	ll
exude	xd	eyelid	ld
exult	xll	eyesight	u

F

fable	fb	factory	fky
fabric	fbk	faculty	$fkll,$
fabricate	$fbka$	fad	fd
fabrication	$fbky$	fade	fd
fabulous	$fblx$	fadeless	fdl'
facade	fsd	fag	fg
face	fas	faggot	fgl
facet	fsl	fail	fl
facetious	fsx	failure	flu
facial	fx	faint	$fa-$
facile	fsl	fair	fa
facilitate	$falla$	fairer	Ja
facility	$fsl)$	fairness	fa'
facsimile	$fks\frown l$	fairy	by
fact	fk	faith	fal
faction	fky	faithful	ll
factious	fkx	faithfulness	ll'
factor	Jk	faithless	fll'

90

Word	Shorthand	Word	Shorthand
fake		far	
falcon		far-away	
fall		farce	
fallacious		farcical	
fallacy		fare	
fallen		farewell	
fallible		farm	
fallow		farmer	
false		farmhouse	
falsetto		farmyard	
falsify		farrier	
falsity		farrow	
falter		farther	
fame		farthest	
familiar		farthing	
familiarize		fascinate	
family		fascination	
famine		fashion	
famish		fashionable	
famous		fast	
famously		fasten	
fan		fastening	
fanatic		faster	
fanaticism		fastidious	
fancy		fat	
fang		fatal	
fantastic		fatalism	
fantasy		fatalistic	

91

fate		February	
father		fecund	
fatherland		fecundity	
fatherless		fed	
fathom		federal	
fathomless		federation	
fatigue		fee	
fatness		feeble	
fatter		feed	
fatuous		feeder	
fault		feel	
faultless		feeling	
faulty		feelings	
favour		feet	
favourable		feign	
favourite		feint	
favouritism		felicitate	
fawn		felicitous	
fealty		felicity	
fear		feline	
fearful		fell	
fearless		fellow	
feasibility		fellowship	
feasible		felon	
feast		felonious	
feat		felony	
feather		felt	
feature		female	

feminine		festivity	
femoral		festoon	
femur		fetch	
fen		fete	
fence		fetid	
fend		fetish	
fender		fetlock	
fennel		fetter	
ferment		feud	
fermentation		feudalism	
fern		fever	
ferocious		feverish	
ferocity		feverishly	
ferret		feverishness	
ferric		few	
ferrule		fewer	
ferry		fiasco	
fertile		fib	
fertility		fibre	
fertilization		fibrous	
fertilize		fickle	
fertilizer		fiction	
fervent		fictitious	
fervour		fiddle	
festal		fidelity	
fester		fidget	
festival		fiduciary	
festive		field	

93

fielder	*Jel*	fillet	*fll*
fiend	*fe—*	fillip	*flp*
fiendish	*fe—3*	filly	*fl,*
fierce	*fers*	film	*fl~*
fierceness	*frs'*	filmy	*fl~,*
fiery	*fy*	filter	*Jl*
fife	*fyf*	filth	*fll*
fifteen	*15*	filthiness	*fll'*
fifteenth	*15l*	filthy	*fll,*
fifth	*5l*	filtrate	*flla*
fiftieth	*50l*	filtration	*fly*
fifty	*50*	fin	*fn*
fig	*fg*	final	*fnl*
fight	*ft*	finally	*fnl*
fighter	*Jt*	finance	*fnv*
figment	*fg—*	financial	*fnx*
figurative	*fgv*	financier	*Jnv*
figure	*fg*	finch	*fc*
figurehead	*fghd*	find	*fe*
filament	*fl—*	finder	*Je*
filbert	*flb/*	fine	*fn*
filch	*flc*	fineness	*fn'*
file	*fl*	finer	*Jn*
filer	*Jl*	finery	*fny*
filial	*fll*	finger	*Jg*
filibuster	*flbs*	finial	*fnl*
filigree	*flge*	finical	*fnK*
fill	*fl*	finish	*fn3*

94

Word	Outline	Word	Outline
finite		fitful	
fir		fitness	
fire		five	5
firearms		fix	
firebrand		fixed	
firefly		fixture	
fireman		flabby	
fireplace		flaccid	
fireproof		flag	
fireside		flagellant	
firkin		flageolet	
firm		flagon	
firmament		flagrant	
firmer		flail	
firmly		flake	
firmness		flamboyant	
first		flame	
first-born		flamingo	
firth		flange	
fiscal		flank	
fish		flannel	
fisher		flannelette	
fisherman		flap	
fishook		flapper	
fissile		flare	
fissure		flash	
fist		flashy	
fit		flask	

95

flat		flight	
flatten		flimsy	
flatter		flinch	
flatterer		fling	
flattery		flint	
flatulent		flinty	
flaunt		flip	
flavour		flippant	
flaw		flirt	
flax		flirtation	
flaxen		flit	
flay		flitch	
flea		float	
flecked		flock	
fled		floe	
fledge		flog	
flee		flood	
fleece		floor	
fleecy		flooring	
fleet		flop	
flesh		floral	
fleshy		florid	
flew		florist	
flexibility		floss	
flexible		flotilla	
flick		flotsam	
flicker		flounce	
flies		flounder	

96

Word	Shorthand	Word	Shorthand
flour		foam	
flourish		fob	
flout		focus	
flow		fodder	
flower		foe	
flowerpot		fog	
flowery		foggy	
fluctuate		fogy	
fluctuation		foible	
flue		foil	
fluency		foist	
fluent		fold	
fluff		folder	
fluid		foliage	
fluidity		foliate	
fluke		foliation	
flung		folio	
flunkey		folk	
fluorescence		follicle	
fluorescent		follow	
flurry		follower	
flush		following	
fluster		folly	
flute		foment	
flutter		fond	
flux		fondle	
fly		fondness	
foal		food	

fool		foregather	
foolish		forefinger	
foolishness		forego	
foolscap		foregone	
foot		foreground	
football		forehead	
footman		foreign	
footprint		foreigner	
footsteps		forejudge	
footstool		foreland	
for		forelock	
forage		foreman	
forbade		forementioned	
forbear		foremost	
forbearance		forenoon	
forbid		forensic	
forbidden		forerunner	
force		foresail	
forceful		foresee	
forcefully		foreshadow	
forcible		foreshorten	
ford		foresight	
fore		forest	
forearm		forestall	
forebode		foretaste	
forecast		foretell	
foreclose		forethought	
foreclosure		foretold	

98

Word	Shorthand	Word	Shorthand
forever		fornication	
forewarn		forsake	
foreword		forsook	
forfeit		forswear	
forfeiture		forsworn	
forgave		fort	
forge		forth	
forgery		forthcoming	
forget		forthwith	
forgetful		fortieth	
forgetfulness		fortification	
forgettable		fortify	
forgive		fortitude	
forgiveness		fortnight	
forgo		fortress	
forgot		fortuitous	
forgotten		fortunate	
fork		fortune	
forlorn		forty	
form		forum	
formal		forward	
formation		forwardness	
formative		fossil	
former		foster	
formerly		fought	
formidable		foul	
formula		found	
formulate		foundation	

Word	Shorthand	Word	Shorthand
founder		framework	
foundling		franc	
fount		France	
fountain		franchise	
four		frank	
fourfold		frankincense	
fourscore		frantic	
fourteen		fraternal	
fourteenth		fraternity	
fourth		fraternize	
fowl		fratricide	
fox		fraud	
foxglove		fraudulent	
foxhound		fraught	
fracas		fray	
fraction		freak	
fractional		freakish	
fractious		freckle	
fracture		free	
fragile		freebooter	
fragility		freedom	
fragment		freehold	
fragmentary		freeman	
fragrance		freer	
fragrant		freethinker	
frail		freeze	
frailty		freight	
frame		French	

Word	Shorthand	Word	Shorthand
frenzy		frisky	
frequency		fritter	
frequent		frivolous	
fresh		frizz	
fresher		fro	
freshman		frock	
freshness		frog	
fret		frolic	
fretful		from	
friable		frond	
friar		front	
fricassee		frontage	
friction		frontal	
Friday		frontier	
fried		frontispiece	
friend		frost	
friendly		frostbitten	
friendship		frosty	
frieze		froth	
frigate		frown	
fright		froze	
frighten		frozen	
frightful		fructiferous	
frigid		fructification	
frigidity		fructify	
frill		frugal	
fringe		frugality	
frisk		frugivorous	

fruit		fundamental	
fruitful		funeral	
fruition		fungus	
fruitless		funicular	
frustrate		funnel	
frustration		funny	
frutescent		fur	
fruticose		furbish	
fry		furious	
fuchsia		furl	
fudge		furlong	
fuel		furlough	
fugitive		furnace	
fugue		furnish	
fulcrum		furniture	
fulfil		furrow	
full		furry	
fully		further	
fulminate		furtherance	
fulness		furthermore	
fulsome		furthermost	
fumble		furthest	
fume		furtive	
fumigate		fury	
fun		fuse	
function		fusible	
functionary		fusillade	
fund		fusion	

fuss		futurist	
fustian		futuristic	
futile		futurity	
future		fuzz	

G

gabardine		gallows	
gabble		galvanic	
gable		galvanism	
gad		galvanize	
gadget		galvanometer	
Gaelic		gamble	
gaff		gambler	
gag		gambol	
gage		game	
gaiety		gammon	
gaily		gamut	
gain		gander	
gaiter		gang	
gale		ganglion	
gall		gangrene	
gallant		gangway	
gallantry		gaol	
galleon		gap	
gallery		gape	
galley		garage	
gallon		garb	
gallop		garbage	

103

garble		gauge	
garden		gaunt	
gardener		gauntlet	
gargle		gauze	
garish		gave	
garland		gavel	
garlic		gavotte	
garment		gawk	
garner		gay	
garnet		gaze	
garnish		gazelle	
garniture		gazette	
garret		gazetteer	
garrison		gear	
garrulous		geese	
garter		gelatin	
gas		gelatinous	
gaseous		geld	
gash		gelid	
gasoline		gem	
gasometer		gender	
gasp		genealogist	
gastric		genealogy	
gastronomy		general	
gate		generality	
gateway		generalization	
gather		generalize	
gaudy		generalship	

generate		geologist	
generation		geology	
generative		geometrical	
generator		geometrician	
generic		geometry	
generosity		georgette	
generous		geranium	
genesis		germ	
genial		German	
genitive		germinate	
genius		germination	
genteel		germinative	
gentian		gerund	
gentility		gesticulate	
gentile		gesticulation	
gentle		gesture	
gentleman		get	
gentlemanly		geyser	
gentlemen		ghastly	
gentleness		gherkin	
gently		ghost	
gentry		ghostly	
genuflexion		ghoul	
genuine		ghoulish	
genus		giant	
geographer		giantess	
geographical		gibber	
geography		gibberish	

gibbet	*jbl*	gist	*J,*
gibe	*μb*	give	*gι*
giblet	*jbl*	given	*gι*
giddy	*gd,*	gizzard	*g3/*
gift	*gf*	glabrous	*gbx*
gig	*gg*	glacial	*gx*
gigantic	*jg-k*	glacier	*gp*
giggle	*ggl*	glad	*gd*
gigolo	*jglo*	gladden	*gdn*
gild	*gld*	glade	*gd*
gill	*gl*	gladiolus	*gdlx*
gill	*jl*	gladly	*gdl*
gillie	*gl,*	gladness	*gd'*
gilt	*gll*	glamour	*g*
gimcrack	*jkk*	glance	*g/*
gimlet	*gll*	gland	*g—*
gin	*jn*	glandular	*g—l*
ginger	*Jj*	glare	*ga*
gingerbread	*Jjbd*	glass	*g'*
gingham	*gg*	glassware	*gs-a*
gipsy	*jps,*	glassy	*gp,*
giraffe	*jf*	glaucous	*gkx*
gird	*q/*	glaze	*g3*
girdle	*q/l*	glazer	*g3*
girl	*q*	glazier	*g3,*
girlish	*gβ*	gleam	*ge*
girt	*q/*	glean	*gn*
girth	*grl*	glebe	*glb*

106

Word	Shorthand	Word	Shorthand
glee		glucose	
gleeful		glue	
glen		glum	
glib		glut	
glide		gluten	
glimmer		glutinous	
glimpse		glutton	
glint		gluttonous	
glisten		gluttony	
glitter		glycerin	
gloaming		gnarl	
gloat		gnash	
globe		gnat	
globular		gnaw	
globule		gnome	
glomerate		go	
gloom		goad	
gloomy		goal	
glorification		goat	
glorify		gobble	
glorious		goblet	
glory		goblin	
gloss		go-cart	
glossary		God	
glossy		goddess	
glove		godfather	
glow		godhead	
glowworm		godlike	

godly		gosling	
godmother		gospel	
goes		gossamer	
goggle		gossip	
going		got	
gold		gouge	
golden		gourd	
goldfinch		gourmand	
goldfish		gourmet	
goldsmith		gout	
golf		govern	
gondola		governess	
gondolier		government	
gone		governor	
gong		gown	
good		grab	
good-bye		grace	
goodliness		graceful	
goodly		gracious	
goodness		gradation	
goodwill		gradient	
goose		grade	
gooseberry		gradual	
gore		gradually	
gorge		graduate	
gorgeous		graduation	
gorilla		graft	
gorse		grain	

Word	Shorthand	Word	Shorthand
grammar		graphology	
grammar school		grapple	
grammatical		grasp	
gramophone		grass	
granary		grasshopper	
grand		grassy	
grandchild		grate	
grandchildren		grateful	
granddaughter		gratification	
grandeur		gratify	
grandfather		gratis	
grandiloquent		gratitude	
grandma		gratuitous	
grandmother		gratuity	
grandparents		grave	
grandson		gravel	
grange		gravely	
granite		graven	
grant		gravestone	
granulate		gravitate	
granulation		gravitation	
granule		gravity	
granulous		gravy	
grape		gray	
grapefruit		grayheaded	
graph		grayness	
graphic		graze	
graphite		grease	

109

Word	Shorthand	Word	Shorthand
greasiness		grieve	
great		grievous	
greater		griffin	
greathearted		grill	
greatness		grim	
greediness		grimace	
greedy		grin	
Greek		grind	
green		grinder	
greener		grindstone	
greenery		grip	
greengage		gripe	
greengrocer		grisly	
greenhorn		grist	
greenhouse		gristle	
greenness		grit	
greenroom		grizzly	
greet		groan	
gregarious		groat	
grenade		grocer	
grenadier		grocery	
grew		grog	
grey		groin	
greyhound		groom	
grid		groove	
griddle		grope	
grief		gross	
grievance		grossest	

Word	Shorthand	Word	Shorthand
grotesque	*(shorthand)*	guard	*(shorthand)*
grotto	*(shorthand)*	guardhouse	*(shorthand)*
ground	*(shorthand)*	guardian	*(shorthand)*
groundhog	*(shorthand)*	guardroom	*(shorthand)*
groundless	*(shorthand)*	guardsman	*(shorthand)*
groundplan	*(shorthand)*	guava	*(shorthand)*
groundwork	*(shorthand)*	gudgeon	*(shorthand)*
group	*(shorthand)*	guerrilla	*(shorthand)*
grouse	*(shorthand)*	guess	*(shorthand)*
grout	*(shorthand)*	guesser	*(shorthand)*
grove	*(shorthand)*	guest	*(shorthand)*
grovel	*(shorthand)*	guidance	*(shorthand)*
grow	*(shorthand)*	guide	*(shorthand)*
grower	*(shorthand)*	guidebook	*(shorthand)*
growl	*(shorthand)*	guidepost	*(shorthand)*
growth	*(shorthand)*	guild	*(shorthand)*
grub	*(shorthand)*	guile	*(shorthand)*
grubby	*(shorthand)*	guileful	*(shorthand)*
grudge	*(shorthand)*	guileless	*(shorthand)*
gruel	*(shorthand)*	guilelessness	*(shorthand)*
gruesome	*(shorthand)*	guillotine	*(shorthand)*
gruff	*(shorthand)*	guilt	*(shorthand)*
grumble	*(shorthand)*	guiltless	*(shorthand)*
grumpy	*(shorthand)*	guilty	*(shorthand)*
grunt	*(shorthand)*	guinea	*(shorthand)*
guano	*(shorthand)*	guise	*(shorthand)*
guarantee	*(shorthand)*	guitar	*(shorthand)*
guarantor	*(shorthand)*	gulf	*(shorthand)*

111

Word	Shorthand	Word	Shorthand
gull		gut	
gullibility		gutter	
gullible		gutteral	
gully		guy	
gulp		guzzle	
gum		gymnasium	
gun		gymnast	
gunboat		gymnastics	
gunner		gypsum	
gunnery		gypsy	
gunpowder		gyrate	
gunwale		gyration	
gurgle		gyroscope	
gush		gyve	
gusset		gyves	
gust			

H

Word	Shorthand	Word	Shorthand
habeas corpus		hackney	
haberdasher		had	
habiliment		haddock	
habit		hag	
habitable		haggard	
habitat		haggle	
habitation		hail	
habitual		hair	
habituate		hairy	
hack		hake	

halcyon		handmade	
hale		handsome	
half		handwriting	
halibut		handy	
hall		hang	
hallow		hanger	
hallucination		hangman	
halo		hanker	
halt		hansom	
halter		haphazard	
halve		hapless	
halyard		happen	
ham		happier	
hamlet		happily	
hammer		happiness	
hammock		happy	
hamper		harangue	
hamstring		harass	
hand		harbinger	
handbill		harbour	
handbook		harbourage	
handcuff		hard	
handful		harden	
handglass		harder	
handicap		hardhearted	
handiwork		hardihood	
handkerchief		hardly	
handle		hardness	

113

Word	Outline	Word	Outline
hardship	h/ʒ	hasp	hs
hardware	h/⌣a	hassock	hsk
hardy	h/,	haste	ha,
hare	ha	hasten	hsn
harem	hr⌣	hastily	hsl
haricot	hyko	hasty	hs,
hark	hrk	hat	hl
harlequin	hrlqn	hatch	hc
harlot	hrll	hatchet	hcl
harm	hr⌣	hatchway	hc⌣a
harmless	hrl'	hate	ha
harmonica	hr⌣nka	hateful	haf
harmonious	hr⌣nx	hatred	hld
harmony	hr⌣n,	haughty	hL,
harness	hr'	haul	hal
harp	hrp	haulage	hlq
harpoon	hrpn	haunch	hac
harpsichord	hrpsk/	haunt	ha-
harpy	hrp,	have	v
harrass	hr'	haven	hʋn
harrow	hro	haversack	Hʋsk
harry	hy	havoc	hʋk
harsh	hrʒ	hawk	hak
harshness	hrʒ'	hawser	Hʒ
hart	h/	hawthorn	hlrn
harvest	hʋ,	hay	ha
has	as	haycock	hkk
hash	hʒ	hazard	hʒ/

114

Word	Shorthand	Word	Shorthand
hazardous	h₃/x	hearty	h/,
haze	h₃	heat	he
hazel	hzl	heater	He
hazy	h₃,	heath	hel
he	h	heathen	hln
head	hd	heave	he
headache	hdk	heaven	hvn 天. 天閝
headlight	hdl	heavenly	hvnl
headlong	hdlq	heavenward	hvn/
headquarters	hdq//	heaver	He
headstrong	hdSq	heavier	Hv,
heal	hel	heavily	hvl
health	hll	heaviness	hv'
healthful	hllf	heavy	hv,
healthier	Hll,	heckle	hK
healthy	hll,	hectic	hkT
heap	hep	hector	Hk
hear	he	hedge	hy
heard	h/	hedgehog	hyhq
hearken	hrkn	hedgerow	hyro
hearsay	hesa	heed	hd
hearse	hrs	heedless	hdl'
heart	h/	heel	hel
heartfelt	h/fl	heifer	hf
hearth	hrl	height	hι
heartily	h/l	heinous	hnx
heartless	h/l'	heir	a
heartlessness	h/"	heiress	a'

115

Word	Shorthand	Word	Shorthand
heirloom		herb	
held		herbaceous	
hell		herbage	
he'll		herd	
hellish		herdsman	
hello		here	
helm		hereafter	
helmet		hereby	
help		hereditary	
helper		heredity	
helpful		herein	
helpless		heresy	
hem		heretic	
hemisphere		herewith	
hemlock		heritage	
hemp		hermetic	
hemstitch		hermit	
hen		hermitage	
hence		hero	
henceforth		heroic	
henceforward		heroine	
henchman		heroism	
hepatic		herring	
heptagon		hers	
her		herself	
herald		hesitate	
heraldic		hesitation	
heraldry		hew	

word	shorthand	word	shorthand
hewer		hinder	
hexagon		hinge	
hexameter		hint	
hiatus		hip	
hibernal		hippodrome	
hiccup		hippopotamus	
hid		hire	
hidden		hireling	
hide		hirsute	
hideous		his	
hiearchy		hiss	
hieratic		histology	
higgle		historian	
high		historic	
higher		historical	
highland		history	
highness		hit	
highroad		hitch	
highway		hither	
hill		hitherto	
hillock		hive	
hillside		hoar	
hilltop		hoard	
hilly		hoarse	
hilt		hoary	
him		hoax	
himself		hobble	
hind		hobby	

117

Word	Shorthand	Word	Shorthand
hock		homesick	
hockey		homeward	
hocus		homicide	
hod		homily	
hoe		homoeopathy	
hog		homologous	
hogshead		homologue	
hoist		homonym	
hold		homosexual	
holder		hone	
hole		honest	
holiday		honesty	
holiness		honey	
hollow		honeycomb	
hollowness		honeymoon	
holly		honeysuckle	
hollyhock		honour	
holm		honourable	
holocaust		honorary	
holograph		hood	
holster		hoodwink	
holt		hoof	
holy		hook	
homage		hoop	
home		hoot	
homeless		hop	
homeliness		hope	
homely		hopeful	

hopeless	hopl'	hostage	hsy
hopelessness	hop"	hostel	hsl
horde	h/	hostelry	hslr,
horizon	hrzn	hostess	hs'
horizontal	hrz-l	hostile	hsl
horn	hrn	hostility	hsl)
hornet	hrnl	hostler	Hsl
hornpipe	hrnpp	hot	hl
horoscope	hrskp	hotel	hll
horrible	hrb	hothouse	hlhs
horrid	hrd	hotter	Hl
horrific	hrfk	hound	h—
horror	Hr	hour	r
horse	hrs	hourly	rl
horseback	hrsbk	house	hs
horsehair	hrsha	household	hshl
horseman	hrsn—	housekeeper	hsKp
horseshoe	hrsZu	housetop	hslp
hortative	h/v	housewife	hsf
horticulture	h/kllu	housework	hsk
horticulturist	h/kllu,	hovel	hvl
hose	hz	hover	Hv
hosiery	hzy	how	h
hospice	hss	however	hv
hospitable	hslb	howitzer	Hls
hospital	hsll	howl	hl
hospitality	hsll)	howsover	hsv
host	ho,	hoyden	hydn

Word	Shorthand	Word	Shorthand
hub		hunch	
hubbub		hundred	
huckster		hundredfold	
huddle		hundredth	
hue		hundredweight	
huff		hung	
hug		hunger	
huge		hungry	
hulk		hunk	
hull		hunt	
hum		hunter	
human		huntsman	
humane		hurdle	
humanism		hurl	
humanity		hurrah	
humankind		hurray	
humble		hurricane	
humdrum		hurry	
humid		hurt	
humidity		hurtful	
humiliate		hurtle	
humiliation		husband	
humility		husbandry	
hummock		hush	
humorist		husk	
humorous		hussar	
humour		hussy	
hump		hustings	

hustle	ħsl	hygienic	ħynk
hut	ħl	hymen	ħmn
hutch	ħc	hymn	ħm
hydrant	H–	hyperbola	ħpbla
hydrate	Hl	hyperbole	ħpbl
hydraulic	Hlk	hyphen	ħfn
hydrocarbon	Hkabn	hypnosis	ħpnss
hydrocephalus	Hflx	hypnotic	ħpnᵀ
hydrogen	Hyn	hypnotism	ħpnlz
hydrometer	Hle	hypnotize	ħpnlz
hydropathic	Hplk	hypochondria	ħpk —— a
hydrophobia	Hfb	hypocrisy	ħpks,
hydroplane	Hpn	hypocrite	ħpkl
hydrostatics	Hᴊ°	hypodermic	Hpᵣk
hydroxide	Hxd	hypotenuse	ħplᵣs
hyena	ħna	hypothesis	ħplss
hygiene	ħyn	hysteria	ħŝa

I

iambic	⌐bk	idea	id
iambus	⌐bx	ideal	idl
ice	is	idealism	idlz
iceberg	isbrq	idealist	idl,
ice-cream	iske	idealize	idelz
icicle	isK	identical	id–K
iconoclasm	ikklz	identically	id–K
iconoclast	ikkl,	identifiable	id–fb
icy	is,	identification	id–f

121

identify		illegible	
identity		illegitimacy	
idiom		illegitimate	
idiosyncrasy		illiberal	
idiot		illicit	
idiotic		illimitable	
idle		illiterate	
idleness		illness	
idler		illogical	
idol		illuminate	
idolatress		illumination	
idolatry		illumine	
idolize		illusion	
idyll		illustrate	
idyllic		illustration	
if		illustrative	
igneous		illustrious	
ignite		image	
ignoble		imagery	
ignominious		imaginable	
ignominy		imaginary	
ignoramus		imagination	
ignorance		imaginative	
ignorant		imagine	
ignore		imbecile	
ill		imbecility	
illegal		imbibe	
illegality		imbroglio	

imbrue	ꓴbu	immolate	ꓴla
imbue	ꓴbu	immoral	vrl
imitable	ꓴb	immorality	vrl)
imitate	ꓴa	immortal	ı/l
imitation	ꓴy	immortality	ı/l)
imitative	ꓴv	immortalize	ı/lʒ
imitator	Ꝺla	immovable	wb
immaculate	ꓴkla	immunity	ꓴn)
immanent	ꓴn–	immure	ꓴu
immaterial	Ꝺal	immutability	ꓴb)
immature	ꓴu	immutable	ꓴb
immeasurable	v/b	imp	ꓴp
immediate	ꓴda	impact	ꓴpk
immemorial	ꓴyl	impair	ꓴpa
immense	✓	impale	ꓴpl
immensity	✓)	impalement	ꓴpl–
immerge	ꓴy	impalpable	ꓴplpb
immerse	ꓴs	impart	ꓴp/
immersion	ꓴy	impartial	ꓴpx
immigrate	ꓴga	impartiality	ꓴpx)
immigrant	ꓴq–	impassability	ꓴpsb)
immigration	ꓴg	impassable	ꓴpsb
imminence	ꓴv	impassible	ꓴpsb
imminent	ꓴn–	impassion	ꓴpy
immobile	ꓴbl	impassive	ꓴpsv
immobility	ꓴbl)	impatience	ꓴpʒ
immoderate	Ꝺda	impatient	ꓴpʒ–
immodest	ꓴd,	impeach	ꓴpc

123

Word	Shorthand	Word	Shorthand
impeccable		impervious	
impecunious		impetuous	
impede		impiety	
impediment		impinge	
impel		impingement	
impend		impious	
impenetrability		impish	
impenetrable		implacability	
impenitent		implacable	
imperative		implant	
imperceptible		implement	
imperfect		implicate	
imperfection		implicit	
imperforate		implore	
imperforation		imploringly	
imperial		imply	
imperialism		impolite	
imperialist		impoliteness	
imperil		impolitic	
imperious		imponderability	
imperishable		imponderable	
impermeable		import	
impersonal		importance	
impersonate		important	
impersonation		importantly	
impertinent		importation	
imperturbability		importer	
imperturbable		importunate	

124

importune		improbable	
importunity		improbity	
impose		impromptu	
imposition		improper	
impossibility		impropriety	
impossible		improve	
impostor		improvement	
imposture		improvidence	
impotence		improvident	
impotent		improvization	
impound		improvize	
impoverish		imprudent	
impracticable		imprudence	
imprecate		impudent	
imprecation		impugn	
impregnable		impulse	
impregnate		impulsive	
impregnation		impunity	
impress		impure	
impressibility		impureness	
impression		impurity	
impressionable		imputation	
impressive		impute	
imprimatur		in	
imprint		inability	
imprison		inaccessibility	
imprisonment		inaccessible	
improbability		inaccuracy	

125

inaccurate	nkua	inaugurate	ngua
inaction	nak	inauguration	nguy
inactivity	nakv)	inauspicious	nasx
inadequacy	ndqs,	inborn	nbrn
inadequate	ndqa	inbred	nbd
inadmissibility	narsb)	incalculable	nklkllb
inadmissible	narsb	incandescent	nk—s-
inadvertent	nav/-	incantation	nk-|
inalienable	nalnb	incapability	nkpb)
inane	nn	incapable	nkpb
inanimate	nana	incapacitate	nkpsla
inanition	nny	incapacity	nkps)
inanity	nn)	incarcerate	nkasa
inapplicability	npkb)	incarceration	nkay
inapplicable	npkb	incarnate	nkana
inappreciable	npßb	incarnation	nkay
inapproachable	npcb	incautious	nkxc
inappropriate	nppa	incendiary	ns—y
inapt	nap	incense	ns/
inaptitude	napld	incentive	ns-v
inarticulate	n/kla	inception	nspy
inartistic	n/S	inceptive	nspv
inasmuch	nsrc	incertitude	ns/ld
inattention	naly	incessant	nss-
inattentive	nal-u	incest	ns,
inaudible	nadb	incestuous	nssx
inaudibly	nadb	inch	un
inaugural	ngul	inchoate	nkoa

126

incident	rsd-	incommensurable	nk/ub
incidental	rsd-l	incommensurate	nk/ua
incinerate	rSra	incommode	rkd
incinerator	rSrax	incommodious	nkdx
incipient	rsp-	incommunicable	rkukb
incise	rs3	incommutable	rkub
incision	rsy	incomparable	rkPb
incisive	rssv	incompatibility	rkplb)
incisively	rssvl	incompatible	rkplb
incisor	rs3	incompetence	rkpl/
incitation	rsiy	incompetency	rkpl/
incite	rsi	incompetent	rkpl-
incitement	rsi-	incomplete	rkpe
incivility	rsvl)	incompleteness	rkpe'
inclemency	nc√	incomprehensibility	rkph/b)
inclement	nc-	incomprehensible	rkph/b
inclination	ncry	incomprehensive	rkph/v
incline	ncn	incompressible	rkpsb
inclined	ncn̄	incomputable	rkpub
include	ncd	inconceivable	rkseb
inclusion	ncq	inconclusive	rkcsv
inclusive	ncsv	incondensable	rkd/b
inclusively	ncsvl	incongruity	rkq)
incognito	rkgrlo	incongrous	rkgx
incognizable	rkgnzb	inconsequent	rksq-
incoherent	rkhe-	inconsiderable	rKsb
incombustible	rkbsb	inconsiderate	rKsa
income	rk	inconsiderateness	rKsa'

English	Shorthand	English	Shorthand
inconsideration		increase	
inconsistence		incredible	
inconsistency		incredulity	
inconsistent		incredulous	
inconsolable		incriminate	
inconspicuous		incrustation	
inconstant		incubate	
inconsumable		incubation	
incontestable		incubator	
incontinent		incubus	
incontinently		inculcate	
incontrovertible		inculcation	
inconvenience		inculpate	
inconvenient		incumbency	
inconvertible		incumbent	
inconvincible		incur	
incorporate		incurable	
incorporation		incursion	
incorporeal		incurvation	
incorrect		incurve	
incorrigibility		indebted	
incorrigible		indebtedness	
incorrodible		indecency	
incorrupt		indecent	
incorruptibility		indecipherable	
incorruptible		indecision	
incorruption		indecisive	
incorruptness		indecorum	

indecorous	*ndkxc*	Indian	*ndn*
indeed	*ndd*	indicate	*ndka*
indefatigable	*ndflgb*	indication	*ndky*
indefatigably	*ndflgb*	indicative	*ndkv*
indefeasible	*ndfzb*	indicator	*ndka*
indefensible	*ndf/b*	indict	*ndi*
indefinable	*ndfub*	indictable	*ndib*
indefinite	*ndfn*	indictment	*ndi –*
indefiniteness	*ndfn'*	indifference	*ndf/*
indelible	*ndllb*	indifferent	*ndf –*
indelicacy	*ndlks,*	indigenous	*ndjnxc*
indelicate	*ndlka*	indigent	*ndy –*
indemnification	*ndnf*	indigestible	*ndjsb*
indemnify	*ndnf*	indigestion	*ndjsy*
indemnity	*ndn)*	indignant	*ndgn –*
indemonstrable	*ndnSb*	indignation	*ndgry*
indent	*nd –*	indignity	*ndgn)*
indentation	*nd –y*	indigo	*ndg*
indenture	*nd – u*	indirect	*ndrk*
independence	*ndp —/*	indiscernible	*ndsnb*
independency	*ndp —/*	indiscreet	*ndske*
independent	*ndp — –*	indiscretion	*ndsky*
indescribable	*ndesb*	indiscriminate	*ndsk na*
indestructible	*ndSkb*	indiscrimination	*ndsk ry*
indeterminable	*nDnb*	indiscriminative	*ndsk nv*
indeterminate	*nDna*	indispensable	*nds/b*
indetermination	*nDy*	indispose	*ndsz*
index	*ndxc*	indisposition	*ndszy*

129

indisputable	inebriation
indissoluble	ineffable
indistinct	ineffaceable
indistinguishable	ineffective
indite	ineffectual
individual	inefficacious
individualism	inefficacy
individuality	inefficiency
indivisible	inefficient
indocility	inelegant
indoctrinate	ineligible
indolence	inept
indolent	ineptitude
indomitable	ineptness
indoors	inequality
indubitable	inequitable
induce	ineradicable
inducement	inert
induct	inertia
induction	inessential
inductive	inestimable
indulge	inevitability
indulgence	inevitable
indurate	inevitably
industrial	inexact
industrious	inexcusable
industry	inexhaustible
inebriate	inexorable

130

Word	Shorthand	Word	Shorthand
inexpedient		inference	
inexperienced		inferior	
inexpressibly		inferiority	
inexpensive		infernal	
inexpiable		infest	
inexplicable		infidel	
inexplicit		infidelity	
inexpressible		infiltrate	
inexpressive		infiltration	
inextinguishable		infinite	
inextricable		infinitesimal	
infallibility		infinitive	
infallible		infinity	
infamous		infirm	
infamy		infirmary	
infancy		infirmity	
infant		inflame	
infanticide		inflammable	
infantile		inflammation	
infantry		inflammatory	
infatuate		inflate	
infatuation		inflect	
infect		inflection	
infection		inflective	
infectious		inflexibility	
infelicitous		inflexible	
infelicity		inflict	
infer		infliction	

131

influence		ingratiate	
influential		ingratitude	
influenza		ingredient	
influx		ingress	
inform		inhabit	
informal		inhabitable	
informality		inhabitant	
informant		inhalation	
information		inhale	
informer		inharmonious	
infraction		inhere	
infrequent		inherence	
infringe		inherent	
infringement		inherit	
infuriate		inheritance	
infuse		inheritor	
infusion		inhibit	
ingather		inhibition	
ingenious		inhibitory	
ingenuity		inhospitable	
ingenuous		inhuman	
ingenuousness		inhumanity	
ingle		inimical	
inglorious		inimitable	
ingot		iniquitous	
ingrain		iniquity	
ingrained		initial	
ingrate		initiate	

initiation		innerve	
initiative		innings	
initiatory		innkeeper	
inject		innocence	
injection		innocent	
injector		innocuous	
injudicious		innovate	
injunction		innovation	
injure		innovator	
injurious		innuendo	
injury		innumerable	
injustice		innutritious	
ink		inobservant	
inkling		inoculate	
inkwell		inoculation	
inlaid		inoffensive	
inland		inoperative	
inlay		inopportune	
inlet		inordinate	
inmate		inorganic	
inmost		inquietude	
inn		inquest	
innate		inquire	
innavigable		inquiry	
inner		inquisition	
innermost		inquisitive	
innervate		inquisitor	
innervation		inquisitorial	

133

Word	Outline	Word	Outline
inroad		insignificance	
insalubrious		insignificant	
insane		insincere	
insanitary		insincerity	
insatiable		insinuate	
insatiate		insinuation	
inscribe		insipid	
inscription		insipidity	
inscriptive		insist	
inscrutable		insistence	
insect		insobriety	
insecure		insolence	
insecurity		insolent	
insensate		insoluble	
insensibility		insolvency	
insensible		insolvent	
insensitive		insomnia	
insentient		insomuch	
inseparability		inspect	
inseparable		inspection	
insert		inspector	
insertion		inspiration	
inshore		inspiratory	
inside		inspire	
insidious		instability	
insidiousness		install	
insight		installation	
insignia		instalment	

instance	insulation
instant	insulator
instantaneous	insult
instantly	insuperable
instead	insupportable
instep	insuppressible
instigate	insurable
instigator	insurance
instillation	insure
instinct	insurgent
instinctive	insurmountable
institute	insurrection
institution	insurrectionary
instruct	insusceptibility
instruction	insusceptible
instructive	intact
instructor	intaglio
instrument	intangibility
instrumental	intangible
instrumentalist	integer
instruments	integral
insubordinate	integrate
insubordination	integrity
insufferable	integument
insufficiency	intellect
insufficient	intellectual
insular	intelligence
insulate	intelligent

135

intelligibility		interest	
intelligible		interfere	
intemperance		interference	
intemperate		interfuse	
intend		interim	
intense		interior	
intensify		interject	
intension		interjection	
intensity		interlace	
intensive		interlard	
intent		interleave	
intention		interline	
inter		interlock	
interact		interlocutor	
intercede		interlope	
intercept		interlude	
intercession		interlunar	
intercessory		intermarriage	
interchange		intermarry	
interchangeable		intermedial	
intercollegiate		intermediary	
intercommunicate		intermediate	
intercommunication		interment	
intercommunion		intermezzo	
intercommunity		interminable	
intercourse		intermingle	
interdict		intermission	
interdictory		intermit	

intermittent	𝑛𝑙-	interstate	𝑛𝑠𝑎
intermix	𝑛𝑥	interstice	𝑛𝑠𝑠
intermixture	𝑛𝑥𝑢	interstitial	𝑛𝑠𝑥
intern	𝑛𝑛	intertwine	𝑛𝑙𝑛
internal	𝑛𝑙	interval	𝑛𝑙
international	𝑛𝑦𝑙	intervene	𝑛𝑛
internationalize	𝑛𝑦𝑙𝑧	intervention	𝑛𝑦
internecine	𝑛𝑠𝑛	interview	𝑛𝑢
internuncio	𝑛°	interweave	𝑛𝑒
interpellate	𝑛𝑝𝑙𝑎	interwoven	𝑛𝑜𝑛
interpellation	𝑛𝑝𝑦	intestacy	𝑛𝑙𝑠𝑠,
interpellator	𝑛𝑝𝑙𝑎𝑟	intestate	𝑛𝑙𝑠𝑎
interpolate	𝑛𝑝𝑙𝑎	intestine	𝑛𝑙𝑠𝑛
interpolation	𝑛𝑝𝑦	intimacy	𝑛𝑙𝑠,
interpose	𝑛𝑝3	intimate	𝑛𝑙𝑎
interposition	𝑛𝑝3𝑦	intimation	𝑛𝑙𝑦
interpret	𝑛𝑝𝑙	intimidate	𝑛𝑙𝑑𝑎
interpretation	𝑛𝑝𝑦	intimidation	𝑛𝑙𝑑𝑦
interpreter	𝑛𝑝𝑙𝑟	into	𝑛𝑙
interregnum	𝑛𝑔𝑛	intolerable	𝑛𝑙𝑙𝑏
interrogate	𝑛𝑔𝑎	intolerance	𝑛𝑙/
interrogation	𝑛𝑔𝑦	intonate	𝑛𝑙𝑎
interrogative	𝑛𝑔𝑣	intonation	𝑛𝑙𝑦
interrogatory	𝑛𝑔𝑙𝑦	intone	𝑛𝑙𝑛
interrupt	𝑛𝑝	intoxicate	𝑛𝑙𝑥𝑘𝑎
interruption	𝑛𝑝𝑦	intoxicant	𝑛𝑙𝑥𝑘-
intersperse	𝑛𝑠𝑠	intractable	𝑛𝑙𝑏
interspersion	𝑛𝑠𝑦	intramural	𝑛𝑙

137

Word	Shorthand	Word	Shorthand
intransitive		invalid	
intravenous		invalidate	
intrepid		invalidity	
intricacy		invaluable	
intricate		invariable	
intrigue		invasion	
intrinsic		invective	
introduce		inveigle	
introduction		inveiglement	
introductory		invent	
intromission		invention	
intromit		inventor	
introspection		inventory	
introspective		inversion	
introversion		invert	
introvert		invertebrate	
intrude		invest	
intrusion		investigate	
intrusive		investigation	
intuition		investiture	
intuitional		investment	
intuitive		inveteracy	
inundate		inveterate	
inundation		invidious	
inure		invigorate	
inutility		invigoration	
invade		invincibility	
invader		invincible	

138

inviolable	‿ⱳᶩᵇ	iron	‿ᴍ
inviolability	‿ⱳᶩᵇ)	ironically	‿ᴍK
inviolate	‿ⱳᶩᵃ	ironmonger	‿ᴍᶫᵠ
invisibility	‿ᴜᵤᵦ)	irony	‿ᴍ,
invisible	‿ᴜᵤᵦ	irradiance	ⱳᵈ/
invitation	‿ⱳᵗ	irradiate	ⱳᵈₐ
invite	‿ᴍ	irrational	ⱳᵧᶩ
invocation	‿ⱳᵏ	irreclaimable	ⱳᶜᵇ
invoice	‿ⱳᵧ	irreconcilable	ⱳᵏₛᶩᵇ
invoke	‿ⱳᵏ	irrecoverable	ⱳKᵤᵦ
involuntary	‿ⱳᶩ–ᵧ	irredeemable	ⱳᵈₑᵇ
involute	‿ⱳᶫᵤ	irreducible	ⱳᵈₛᶩ
involution	‿ⱳᶩ	irrefragable	ⱳᵮᵧᵇ
involve	‿ⱳᶫᵥ	irrefrangible	ⱳᵮᵦ
invulnerability	ᴺᶫⱳᵇ)	irrefutable	ⱳᵮᵤᵇ
invulnerable	ᴺᶫⱳᵇ	irregular	ⱳₑᵠ
inward	ᴺ/	irregularity	ⱳₑᵠ)
inweave	ⱳₑ	irrelevancy	ⱳᶩᵥ
inwrought	ⱳᶫ	irrelevant	ⱳᶩᵥ–
iodine	ⱳᵈᴍ	irreligion	ⱳᶩ
iota	ⱳₐ	irremediable	ⱳᵈᵇ
irascible	ⱳₛᵇ	irremovable	ⱳⱳᵇ
irate	ᵀₐ	irreparable	ⱳᵖᵇ
ire	ᵀ	irreprehensible	ⱳᵖʰ/ᵇ
Ireland	ᵀᶩ —	irrepressible	ⱳᵖₛᵇ
iris	ᵀᴖ	irreproachable	ⱳᵖᶜᵇ
Irish	ᵀᵦ	irresistible	ⱳᵤₛᵇ
irksome	ᵀₖₛ	irresolute	ⱳᵤᶩᵤ

139

irresolution		isolate	
irrespective		isolation	
irresponsible		isosceles	
irretrievable		issuance	
irreverent		issue	
irreversible		isthmus	
irrevocable		it	
irrigate		itch	
irrigation		item	
irritable		iterate	
irritant		iteration	
irritate		itinerant	
irritation		itinerary	
irritative		itinerate	
irruption		its	
irruptive		itself	
is		ivory	
island		ivy	
isle			

J

jab		jade	
jabber		jag	
jacinth		jagged	
jack		jaggedness	
jackal		jaguar	
jackass		jail	
jacket		jailer	

Word	Shorthand	Word	Shorthand
jailor		jet	
jam		jewel	
jamb		jeweller	
jangle		jewellery	
janitor		jib	
January		jig	
jar		jilt	
jargon		jingle	
jasmine		job	
jasper		jockey	
jaundice		jocose	
jaunt		jocular	
javelin		jocularity	
jaw		jocularly	
jay		jocund	
jealous		jog	
jealousy		join	
jeans		joint	
jeer		jointure	
jeerer		joist	
jejune		joke	
jelly		jollification	
jeopardize		jollity	
jeopardy		jolly	
jerk		jolt	
jerkin		jostle	
jersey		jot	
jest		journal	

141

word	shorthand	word	shorthand
journalism		juggler	
journalist		jugular	
journalistic		juice	
journey		juicy	
journeyman		julep	
joust		July	
jovial		jumble	
joviality		jump	
jowl		jumper	
joy		junction	
joyful		juncture	
joyless		June	
joyous		jungle	
jubilant		junior	
jubilation		juniority	
jubilee		juniper	
judge		junk	
judgement		junket	
judicable		juridical	
judicative		jurisdiction	
judicatory		jurisprudence	
judicature		jurist	
judicial		juror	
judiciary		jury	
judicious		juryman	
judiciousness		just	
jug		justice	
juggle		justiciable	

142

justiciary		jut	
justifiable		jute	
justification		juvenile	
justify		juxtaposition	
justness			

K

kail		keystone	
kangaroo		khaki	
kayak		kick	
kedge		kid	
keel		kidnap	
keen		kidnapper	
keenness		kidney	
keep		kill	
keeper		kiln	
keepsake		kilo	
keg		kilogram	
kelp		kilometre	
ken		kilt	
kennel		kimono	
kept		kin	
kernel		kind	
kerosene		kinder	
kestrel		kindergarten	
ketchup		kindle	
kettle		kindling	
key		kindly	

143

Word	Outline	Word	Outline
kindness	ki'	knead	nd
kindred	k—d	knee	ne
king	kq	kneel	nel
kingdom	kgd	knell	nl
kingly	kgl	knelt	nll
kinsfolk	knzfk	knew	nu
kinsman	knz—	knickers	nks
kinship	knʒ	knife	nf
kipper	Kp	knight	ne
kirk	krk	knighthood	nehd
kiss	k'	knightly	nel
kit	kl	knit	nl
kitchen	kcn	knives	nus
kite	ki	knob	nb
kith	kl	knock	nk
kitten	kln	knoll	nol
kitty	k)	knot	nl
kleptomania	kpna	know	no
knack	nk	knowing	no
knap	np	knowledge	nlg
knapsack	npsk	known	no
knave	na	knuckle	nK
knavery	nay	kosher	Kʒ
knavish	naʒ		

L

Word	Outline	Word	Outline
label	lb	labour	lab
labial	lbl	laboratory	lbly

labourer	*Labr*	lair	*la*
laborious	*llyx*	laird	*la/*
labyrinth	*lbnl*	laity	*la)*
lace	*las*	lake	*lk*
lacerate	*lsa*	lamb	*ʰ*
laceration	*lsy*	lambent	*lb-*
lacerative	*lsv*	lame	*la*
lachrymal	*lkrl*	lament	*l-*
lack	*lk*	lamentable	*l-b*
lackadaisical	*lkdʒk*	lamentation	*l-ɪ*
lackey	*lk,*	laminate	*lna*
laconic	*lkk*	lamination	*lny*
lacquer	*lk*	lamp	*lp*
lacrosse	*lk'*	lampoon	*lpn*
lactation	*lky*	lamprey	*lpa*
lactic	*lkᴛ*	lance	*V*
lacuna	*lkna*	lancet	*V l*
lad	*ld*	land	*l—*
ladder	*la*	landau	*l—a*
ladies	*ld,,*	landlord	*l—l/*
lading	*l̲d̲*	landmark	*l—rk*
ladle	*ldl*	landscape	*l—skp*
lady	*ld,*	landward	*l—/*
lag	*lq*	lane	*ln*
laggard	*lq/*	language	*lgl*
lagoon	*lgn*	languid	*lgd*
laid	*ld*	languish	*lgβ*
lain	*ln*	lank	*lq*

Word	Outline	Word	Outline
lantern	l-ɹn	lathe	lal
lanyard	lny/	lather	La
lap	lp	Latin	l̲n
lapidary	lpdy	latitude	lttd
lapse	lps	latitudinal	lttdnl
larceny	bsn,	latter	ll
larch	brc	lattice	lls
lard	l/	laud	lad
large	lʒ	laudable	ldb
largeness	lʒ'	laudanum	ldn
larger	lʒ	laudatory	ldly
largesse	lʒ'	laugh	ll
lark	brk	laughable	llb
larkspur	brksr	laughter	ll
larva	bva	launch	lac
lascivious	lsvc	launder	l—
lash	lʒ	laundress	l—'
lass	l'	laundry	l—,
lassitude	lsld	laureate	lya
last	l,	laurel	brl
latch	lc	lava	lva
late	la	lavatory	lvly
lately	lal	lavender	lv—
lateness	la'	lavish	lvʒ
latent	la-	lavishness	lvʒ'
later	la	law	la
lateral	lll	lawful	laf
lath	ll	lawgiver	laʄ

146

lawless	*lal'*	leash	*leʒ*
lawmaker	*laⁿk*	least	*le,*
lawn	*lan*	leather	*Le*
lawyer	*La* *La*	leathern	*Len*
laxative	*lxv*	leave	*le*
laxity	*lx)*	leaven	*lun*
lay	*la*	leaves	*les*
layer	*La*	lecherous	*Lcx*
layette	*lal*	lectern	*lkrn*
layman	*lan-*	lecture	*lku*
lazy	*l₃,*	lecturer	*Lku*
lead	*ld*	lectureship	*lkuʒ*
leaden	*ldn*	led	*ld*
leader	*Ld*	ledge	*l₄*
leadership	*Ldʒ*	ledger	*l₄*
leaf	*lal*	lee	*le*
leafage	*lff*	leech	*lec*
leafless	*lffl'*	leek	*lek*
leafy	*lf,*	leer	*le*
league	*leq*	leeway	*lea*
leaguer	*Lq*	left	*lf*
leak	*lek*	leg	*lq*
leakage	*lk₁*	legacy	*lqs,*
lean	*ln*	legal	*lql*
leap	*lep*	legality	*lql)*
learn	*ln*	legalization	*lqlₓ₁*
learner	*Ln*	legalize	*lql₃*
lease	*les*	legate	*lqa*

Word	Shorthand	Word	Shorthand
legatee		lent	
legation		lentil	
legend		leonine	
legendary		leopard	
leggings		leper	
legibility		leprosy	
legible		leprous	
legion		lesbian	
legionary		lesion	
legislate		less	
legislation		lessen	
legislative		lesser	
legislature		lesson	
legitimacy		lest	
legitimate		let	
leisure		lethal	
lemon		lethargic	
lemonade		lethargical	
lend		lethargy	
lender		letter	
length		letterhead	
lengthen		letterpress	
lengthier		lettuce	
lengthways		levee	
lengthwise		level	
leniency		lever	
lenient		leverage	
lens		leveret	

leviable	*(shorthand)*	lice	*(shorthand)*
leviathan	*(shorthand)*	licence	*(shorthand)*
levity	*(shorthand)*	license	*(shorthand)*
levy	*(shorthand)*	licentiate	*(shorthand)*
lewd	*(shorthand)*	licentious	*(shorthand)*
lewdness	*(shorthand)*	lichen	*(shorthand)*
lexicographer	*(shorthand)*	lick	*(shorthand)*
lexicography	*(shorthand)*	licorice	*(shorthand)*
lexicologist	*(shorthand)*	lid	*(shorthand)*
lexicology	*(shorthand)*	lie	*(shorthand)*
lexicon	*(shorthand)*	lief	*(shorthand)*
liability	*(shorthand)*	liege	*(shorthand)*
liable	*(shorthand)*	lien	*(shorthand)*
liaison	*(shorthand)*	lieu	*(shorthand)*
liar	*(shorthand)*	lieutenant	*(shorthand)*
libation	*(shorthand)*	life	*(shorthand)*
libel	*(shorthand)*	lifeless	*(shorthand)*
libellous	*(shorthand)*	lifelong	*(shorthand)*
liberal	*(shorthand)*	lifetime	*(shorthand)*
liberality	*(shorthand)*	lift	*(shorthand)*
liberalize	*(shorthand)*	ligament	*(shorthand)*
liberate	*(shorthand)*	ligature	*(shorthand)*
libertine	*(shorthand)*	light	*(shorthand)*
liberty	*(shorthand)*	lighten	*(shorthand)*
libidinous	*(shorthand)*	lighter	*(shorthand)*
librarian	*(shorthand)*	lighthouse	*(shorthand)*
library	*(shorthand)*	lightly	*(shorthand)*
libretto	*(shorthand)*	lightness	*(shorthand)*

lightning	*(shorthand)*	lineage	*(shorthand)*
lightship	*(shorthand)*	lineal	*(shorthand)*
like	*(shorthand)*	lineament	*(shorthand)*
likeable	*(shorthand)*	linear	*(shorthand)*
likely	*(shorthand)*	linen	*(shorthand)*
liken	*(shorthand)*	liner	*(shorthand)*
likeness	*(shorthand)*	linger	*(shorthand)*
likewise	*(shorthand)*	lingerie	*(shorthand)*
lilac	*(shorthand)*	lingo	*(shorthand)*
lilt	*(shorthand)*	lingual	*(shorthand)*
lily	*(shorthand)*	linguist	*(shorthand)*
limb	*(shorthand)*	linguistic	*(shorthand)*
limber	*(shorthand)*	liniment	*(shorthand)*
limbo	*(shorthand)*	lining	*(shorthand)*
lime	*(shorthand)*	link	*(shorthand)*
limekiln	*(shorthand)*	linnet	*(shorthand)*
limelight	*(shorthand)*	linoleum	*(shorthand)*
limestone	*(shorthand)*	Linotype	*(shorthand)*
limit	*(shorthand)*	linseed	*(shorthand)*
limitation	*(shorthand)*	lint	*(shorthand)*
limitless	*(shorthand)*	lintel	*(shorthand)*
limousine	*(shorthand)*	lion	*(shorthand)*
limp	*(shorthand)*	lioness	*(shorthand)*
limpet	*(shorthand)*	lip	*(shorthand)*
limpid	*(shorthand)*	liquefaction	*(shorthand)*
linch-pin	*(shorthand)*	liquefy	*(shorthand)*
linden	*(shorthand)*	liqueur	*(shorthand)*
line	*(shorthand)*	liquid	*(shorthand)*

150

liquidate	*lqda*	litigious	*llyx*
liquidation	*lqdy*	litmus	*llrx*
liquidator	*lqda*	litre	*le*
liquor	*lk*	litter	*l*
lisle	*lil*	little	*ll*
lisp	*ls*	littoral	*ll*
lissom	*lsn*	liturgy	*ly,*
list	*l,*	live	*lv*
listen	*lsn*	livelihood	*lvlhd*
listener	*lsn*	livelong	*lvlq*
listless	*lsl'*	lively	*lvl*
lit	*ll*	liver	*lv*
litany	*lln,*	livery	*lvy*
literacy	*ls,*	livestock	*lvsk*
literal	*ll*	livid	*lvd*
literally	*ll*	lizard	*lz/*
literary	*ly*	llama	*lra*
literate	*la*	load	*ld*
literature	*llu*	loadline	*ldl*
lithe	*lil*	loaf	*lof*
lithesome	*lsn*	loam	*lo*
lithograph	*llgf*	loan	*ln*
lithographer	*llgf*	loath	*lol*
lithographic	*llgfk*	loathe	*lol*
lithography	*llgf,*	loathsome	*lsn*
litigant	*llq-*	loaves	*los*
litigate	*llga*	lobby	*lb,*
litigation	*llgy*	lobe	*lob*

151

lobster		loiter	
local		London	
locality		Londoner	
localization		lone	
localize		loneliness	
locate		lonely	
location		lonesome	
loch		long	
lock		longevity	
locket		longhand	
lock-jaw		longitude	
locksmith		longitudinal	
locomotive		look	
locust		lookout	
lode		loom	
lodestar		loop	
lodge		loose	
lodging		loosen	
lodgement		loot	
loft		lop	
lofty		loquacious	
log		loquacity	
logarithm		lord	
loggerhead		lordly	
logic		lordship	
logical		lore	
logician		lorry	
loin		lose	

Word	Shorthand	Word	Shorthand
loser		lubricant	
losing		lubricate	
loss		lubricator	
lost		lucent	
lot		lucid	
lotion		lucidity	
lotus		luck	
loud		luckless	
louder		lucky	
loudly		lucrative	
lounge		lucre	
louse		ludicrous	
lout		lug	
louvre		luggage	
lovable		lugubrious	
love		lukewarm	
loveliness		lull	
lovely		lullaby	
lover		lumbago	
low		lumber	
lower		lumberman	
lowland		luminary	
lowliness		luminosity	
lowly		luminous	
loyal		lump	
loyalist		lunacy	
loyalty		lunar	
lozenge		lunate	

153

lunatic		lusty	
lunch		luxuriant	
luncheon		luxuriate	
lung		luxurious	
lunge		luxury	
lupine		lying	
lurch		lymph	
lure		lymphatic	
lurid		lynch	
lurk		lynx	
luscious		lyre	
lush		lyric	
lust		lyrical	
lustre			

M

ma		madam	
macaroni		madden	
macaroon		made	
macaw		mademoiselle	
mace		madness	
macerate		madrigal	
machination		magazine	
machine		magenta	
machinery		maggot	
machinist		magic	
mackerel		magical	
mad		magician	

154

English	Shorthand	English	Shorthand
magisterial		majestic	
magistrate		majesty	
magnanimity		major	
magnanimous		majority	
magnate		make	
magnesia		maker	
magnet		maladministration	
magnetism		malady	
magnetize		malaria	
magneto		malcontent	
magnificence		male	
magnificent		malediction	
magnify		malefactor	
magniloquent		malevolent	
magnitude		malformation	
magnolia		malice	
magpie		malicious	
mahogany		malign	
maid		malignant	
maiden		malignity	
maidenhood		mall	
mail		mallard	
maim		malleable	
main		mallet	
mainland		mallow	
maintain		malpractice	
maintenance		malt	
maize		maltreat	

155

mamma	⌢a	manifold	⌢fol
mammal	⌢l	manila	⌢la
mammoth	⌢l	manipulate	⌢pla
mammy	⌢,	mankind	⌢ki
man	⌢-	manly	⌢l
manacle	⌢K	manna	⌢a
manage	⌢y	manner	⋀n
management	⌢y-	mannerism	⋀z
manager	⌢gr	manoeuvre	⋀v
mandarin	⋀— n	manor	⋀n
mandate	⌢— a	manse	⟍
mandatory	⌢— ay	mansion	⟍
mandible	⌢— b	manslaughter	⌢sla
mandolin	⌢— ln	mantel	⌢-l
mane	⌢n	mantle	⌢-l
manful	⌢ʃ	manual	⌢ul
mange	⌐y	manufacture	⌐fr
manger	⋀y	manufacturer	⋀fr
mangle	⌢gl	manure	⌢u
mango	⌢go	manuscript	⌢/s
mangrove	⌢ngo	many	⌢
mangy	⌐y,	map	⌢p
manhood	⌢hd	maple	⌢p
mania	⌢a	mar	⌢a
maniac	⌢k	maraud	⌢d
manicure	⌢ku	marble	⌢b
manifest	⌢ʃ,	March	⌐c
manifestation	⌢fʃ	marchioness	⌢y'

156

Word	Outline	Word	Outline
mare		marshy	
margarine		mart	
margin		martial	
marigold		martin	
marine		martinet	
mariner		martyr	
marionette		marvel	
marital		marvellous	
maritime		masculine	
marjoram		mash	
mark		mask	
marker		mason	
market		masonry	
marketable		masquerade	
marketplace		mass	
marl		massacre	
marmalade		massage	
marmoset		massive	
marmot		massy	
maroon		mast	
marquee		master	
marquess		masterful	
marriage		masterpiece	
married		mastery	
marrow		masticate	
marry		mastication	
marsh		mastiff	
marshal		mat	

157

Word	Outline	Word	Outline
matador		maximum	
match		may	
matchless		May	
mate		maybe	
material		mayor	
materialism		mayoress	
materialist		maypole	
maternal		maze	
maternity		mazurka	
mathematician		me	
mathematics		mead	
matricide		meadow	
matriculate		meagre	
matriculation		meal	
matrimonial		mean	
matrimony		meander	
matrix		meaner	
matron		meanness	
matter		meant	
mattress		meantime	
mature		meanwhile	
maturity		measles	
maudlin		measurable	
maul		measure	
mausoleum		measurement	
mauve		meat	
mawkish		mechanic	
maxim		mechanical	

158

Word	Shorthand	Word	Shorthand
mechanism		megaphone	
medal		melancholy	
medalist		meliorate	
medallion		mellifluent	
meddle		mellifluous	
meddler		mellow	
meddlesome		melodious	
medial		melodrama	
mediate		melodramatic	
mediation		melody	
mediator		melon	
medical		melt	
medicate		member	
medication		membership	
medicinal		membrane	
medicine		memento	
mediocre		memoir	
mediocrity		memorable	
meditate		memorandum	
meditation		memorial	
meditative		memorize	
medium		memory	
medlar		men	
medley		menace	
meek		menagerie	
meeker		mend	
meekness		mendacious	
meet		mendacity	

Word	Shorthand	Word	Shorthand
mendicant		mermaid	
menial		merriment	
meningitis		merry	
menstruation		mesh	
mensuration		mesmerize	
mental		mess	
mentality		message	
mention		messenger	
mentor		met	
menu		metal	
mercantile		metallic	
mercenary		metalliferous	
mercerize		metallurgy	
merchandise		metamorphic	
merchant		metaphor	
merchantman		metaphysician	
merciful		metaphysics	
merciless		mete	
mercury		metempsychosis	
mercy		meteor	
mere		meteorite	
merely		meteorologist	
meretricious		meteorology	
merge		meter	
meridian		method	
merino		methodical	
merit		methylated	
meritorious		metric	

metronome		migration	
metropolis		milch	
metropolitan		mild	
mettle		mildness	
miasma		mile	
mica		mileage	
mice		milestone	
microbe		military	
microcosm		militate	
micrometer		militia	
microphone		milk	
microscope		milkmaid	
mid		milkman	
midday		milky	
middle		mill	
midge		millennium	
midnight		miller	
midst		millet	
midsummer		milliard	
midway		millinery	
midwinter		million	
mien		millionaire	
might		millions	
mightier		millstone	
mightiest		mimeograph	
mightily		mimic	
mighty		mimicry	
migrate		minaret	

Word	Outline	Word	Outline
mince		minuteness	
mind		minx	
mindful		miracle	
mine		miraculous	
miner		mirage	
mineral		mire	
mineralist		mirror	
mineralize		mirth	
mineralogist		misadventure	
mineralogy		misadvised	
mingle		misalliance	
miniature		misanthrope	
minimize		misanthropist	
minimum		misanthropy	
minion		misapply	
minister		misapprehend	
ministerial		misapprehension	
ministration		misappropriate	
ministry		misappropriation	
mink		misarrange	
minnow		misarrangement	
minor		misbehave	
minority		misbehaviour	
minster		misbelieve	
minstrel		miscalculate	
mint		miscalculation	
minus		miscall	
minute		miscarry	

162

miscellaneous	~usc	misjudge	~sy
miscellany	~sln,	misjudgment	~sy-
mischance	~sc/	mislay	~sla
mischief	~scf	mislead	~sld
mischievous	~scvx	misled	~sld
misconceive	~skse	mismanage	~smy
misconception	~skspy	mismanagement	~smy-
misconduct	~skdk	misname	~sna
misconstruction	~skSky	misnomer	~sno
misconstrue	~skSu	misogamist	~sg~,
miscount	~skl	misogynist	~syn,
miscreant	~ske-	misplace	~spl
misdirect	~sdrk	misprint	~sp-
misdirection	~sdrky	mispronounce	~sprv
miser	~3	misproportion	~sppy
miserable	~3b	misquotation	~sqq
miserly	~3l	misread	~srd
misery	~34	misreckon	~srkn
misfit	~sfl	misrelate	~srla
misfortune	~sf/n	misreport	~srp/
misgiving	~sg_	misrepresent	~srep
misgovern	~sgvvn	misrepresentation	~srepy
misgovernment	~sgvl	misrule	~srl
misguide	~sgd	miss	~'
mishap	~shp	missal	~sl
misinform	~snf~	mis-shape	~sZp
misinterpret	~sNpl	missile	~sl
misinterpretation	~sNply	mission	~y

missionary	⌒y⌉	mobile	⌒bl
mis-spent	⌒ss-	mobilization	⌒bʒı
mis-state	⌒ssa	mobilize	⌒bʒ
mist	⌒,	moccasin	⌒ksn
mistake	⌒sk	mock	⌒k
mistletoe	⌒sllo	mockery	⌒ky
mistranslate	⌒sꟼla	mode	⌒d
mistranslation	⌒sꟼlↄ	model	⌒dl
mistress	⌒S'	moderate	⌒da
mistrust	⌒S,	modern	⌒dɾn
mistrustful	⌒Ssf	modernize	⌒dɾnʒ
misty	⌒s,	modest	⌒d,
misunderstand	⌒slls—	modesty	⌒ds,
misuse	⌒sus	modicum	⌒dk
mite	⌒ι	modification	⌒df
mitigate	⌒lga	modify	⌒df
mitigation	⌒lgı	modish	⌒dβ
mitigator	⌒lga	modiste	⌒d,
mitre	⌒ι	modulate	⌒dla
mitten	⌒ln	modulation	⌒dlↄ
mix	⌒x	modulator	⌒dla
mixer	⌒x	mohair	⌒ha
mixing	⌒x̱	moist	⌒ɥ,
mixture	⌒xu	moisten	⌒ɥsn
mizzen	⌒ʒn	moisture	⌒ɥsu
moan	⌒n	molar	⌒l
moat	⌒o	molasses	⌒lss
mob	⌒b	mole	⌒ol

164

molecular	$\Omega l l l$	monoplane	$\sim npn$
molecule	$\sim l l l$	monopolize	$\sim npl_{7}$
molest	$\sim l,$	monopoly	$\sim npl$
molestation	$\sim ly$	monosyllable	$\sim nsll$
mollify	$\sim lf$	monotheist	$\sim nle,$
mollusc	$\sim lsk$	monotone	$\sim nln$
molten	$\sim lln$	monotonous	$\sim nlnx$
moment	$\sim o-$	monsoon	$\sim nsn$
momentarily	$\sim o-yl$	monster	$\sim nb$
momentary	$\sim o-y$	monstrosity	$\sim nbs)$
momentous	$\sim o-x$	monstrous	$\sim nbx$
momentum	$\sim o-\sim$	month	$\sim o$
monarch	$\sim nrk$	monthly	$\sim ol$
monarchy	$\sim nrk,$	monument	$\sim n-$
monastery	$\sim nb,$	monumental	$\sim n-l$
monastic	$\sim nS$	mood	$\sim d$
Monday	$\sim n$	moody	$\sim d,$
money	$\sim n,$	moon	$\sim n$
mongrel	$\sim gl$	moonbeam	$\sim nbe$
monitor	$\sim nl$	moonlight	$\sim nl$
monk	$\sim q$	moonshine	$\sim n\zeta n$
monkey	$\sim q,$	moor	$\sim u$
monochrome	$\sim nko$	moorage	$\sim uy$
monogamy	$\sim ng\sim,$	moorish	$\sim u\zeta$
monography	$\sim ngl,$	moorland	$\sim ul-$
monolith	$\sim nll$	moose	$\sim us$
monologue	$\sim nlq$	mop	$\sim p$
monomania	$\sim n n na$	mope	$\sim op$

165

moral		mortuary	
moralist		mosaic	
morality		mosque	
moralize		mosquito	
morass		moss	
morbid		most	
morbidity		mote	
mordant		moth	
more		mother	
moreover		motherhood	
morganatic		motif	
morgue		motion	
moribund		motionless	
morn		motive	
morning		motley	
morocco		motor	
moron		motorcycle	
morose		motorist	
morphia		motorman	
morphine		mottle	
morsel		motto	
mortal		mould	
mortality		moulder	
mortar		mouldy	
mortgage		moult	
mortification		mound	
mortify		mount	
mortise		mountain	

mountaineer		muffle	
mountainous		muffler	
mourn		mufti	
mourner		mug	
mournful		muggy	
mourning		mulberry	
mouse		mule	
moustache		muleteer	
mouth		mull	
mouthful		mullet	
movable		mulligatawny	
move		mullion	
movement		multifarious	
mover		multiform	
mow		multigraph	
mower		multiple	
mown		multiplication	
Mr		multiply	
Mrs		multitude	
much		mum	
mucilage		mumble	
muck		mummy	
mucus		mumps	
mud		munch	
muddle		mundane	
muddy		municipal	
muff		municipality	
muffin		munificence	

muniment	⌒n –	mute	⌒u
munition	⌒y	mutilate	⌒lla
mural	⌒rl	mutilation	⌒lly
murder	/\/	mutilator	/\lla
murderer	/\/r	mutineer	⌒lne
murderous	/\/x	mutinous	⌒lnx
murky	⌒rk,	mutiny	⌒ln,
murmur	/\r⌒	mutter	/\u
muscle	⌒rl	mutton	⌒ln
muscular	/\skl	mutual	⌒uul
muse	⌒3	muzzle	⌒zl
museum	⌒z⌒	my	⌒u
mushroom	⌒Zr⌒	myopia	⌒lpa
music	⌒zk	myriad	⌒yd
musical	⌒zK	myrrh	⌒r
musician	⌒z/	myrtle	⌒/l
musk	⌒sk	myself	⌒us/
musket	⌒skl	mysterious	⌒Sx
musketeer	⌒skle	mystery	⌒S,
musketry	⌒skl,	mystic	⌒S
muskrat	⌒skrl	mystical	⌒sK
muslin	⌒zln	mystification	⌒sf
mussel	⌒sl	mystify	⌒sf
must	⌒,	myth	⌒l
mustard	⌒Sd	mythical	⌒lK
muster	⌒S	mythologist	⌒lol,
mutable	⌒ub	mythology	⌒lol
mutableness	⌒ub'		

N

Word	Shorthand	Word	Shorthand
nab	nb	nation	ry
nadir	nd	national	ryl
nag	nq	nationalism	rylz
nail	nal	nationalist	ryl,
naive	nue	nationality	ryl)
naked	nkd	nationalize	rylz
nakedness	nkd '	native	nv
name	na	nativity	nv)
nameless	nal '	natural	nal
namely	nal	naturalist	nal ,
namesake	nask	naturalization	nalzy
nap	np	naturalize	nalz
nape	nap	nature	na
naphtha	nfla	naught	nal
napkin	npkn	naughty	nl ,
narcissus	nrissx	nausea	nsa
narcotic	nrk	nauseous	nsx
narrate	nra	nautical	nlK
narration	nry	naval	nvl
narrative	nrv	nave	na
narrow	nro	navigable	nvgb
narrowness	nro '	navigate	nvga
nasal	nzl	navigation	nvgy
nasturtium	nsz	navigator	nvga
nasty	ns,	navy	nv,
natal	nll	near	ne

nearby		negative	
nearly		neglect	
nearness		negligence	
neat		negligent	
neatness		negotiable	
nebulous		negotiate	
necessarily		negotiation	
necessary		negotiator	
necessitate		negro	
necessitous		negroid	
necessity		neigh	
neck		neighbour	
necklace		neighbourhood	
necktie		neither	
necrology		neophyte	
necromancy		nephew	
necropolis		nepotism	
necrosis		nerve	
nectar		nerveless	
nectarine		nervous	
need		nervousness	
needful		nest	
needle		nestle	
needless		net	
needlewoman		nettle	
needy		network	
nefarious		neuralgia	
negate		neuralgic	

neuritis		nigh	
neurotic		night	
neuter		nightcap	
neutral		nightfall	
neutrality		nightgown	
neutralization		nightingale	
neutralize		nightly	
never		nightmare	
nevertheless		nimble	
new		nimbus	
newborn		nine	
newcomer		nineteen	
news		nineteenth	
newspaper		ninety	
newt		nip	
next		nipple	
nib		nit	
nibble		nitrate	
nice		nitre	
nicely		nitric	
nicer		nitrogen	
niche		nitrous	
nick		no	
nickel		nobility	
nickname		noble	
nicotine		nobleman	
niece		nobly	
niggardly		nobody	

Word	Shorthand	Word	Shorthand
nocturnal		noose	
nocturne		nor	
nod		normal	
node		north	
noggin		northeast	
noise		northeastern	
noiseless		northerly	
noisier		northern	
noisily		northward	
noisy		northwest	
nomad		northwestern	
nomenclature		nose	
nominal		nostril	
nominate		not	
nomination		notable	
nominator		notably	
nonchalance		notary	
nonchalant		notation	
nondescript		notch	
none		note	
nonentity		noteworthy	
nonpareil		nothing	
nonsense		notice	
nonsensical		noticeable	
noodle		notification	
nook		notify	
noon		notion	
noonday		notoriety	

172

notorious		numb	
notwithstanding		number	
nought		numberless	
noun		numbness	
nourish		numerable	
nourishment		numeral	
novel		numerate	
novelist		numeration	
novelty		numerator	
November		numeric	
novice		numerical	
novitiate		numerous	
now		nun	
nowadays		nunnery	
nowhere		nuptial	
nozzle		nurse	
nuclear		nursery	
nucleus		nurture	
nude		nut	
nudge		nutmeg	
nudity		nutriment	
nugget		nutrition	
nuisance		nutritious	
null		nutritive	
nullification		nutty	
nullify		nymph	
nullity			

173

oak	*ok*	obligatory	*obgly*
oakum	*ok*	oblige	*obj*
oar	*o*	oblique	*obq*
oasis	*oss*	obliterate	*Oba*
oat	*ot*	obliteration	*Oj*
oath	*ot*	oblivion	*obvn*
oatmeal	*otl*	oblivious	*obvx*
obduracy	*obdus,*	oblong	*obg*
obdurate	*obdua*	obloquy	*obq,,*
obedience	*obd/*	obnoxious	*obnkx*
obedient	*obd—*	obscene	*obsn*
obeisance	*obs/*	obscenity	*obsn)*
obelisk	*obsk*	obscure	*obsku*
obese	*obs*	obscurity	*obsku)*
obeseness	*obs'*	obsequies	*obsqB*
obesity	*obs)*	obsequious	*obsqx*
obey	*oba*	observance	*obsv/*
obituary	*obly*	observant	*obsv—*
object	*ob*	observation	*obsuj*
objection	*obj*	observe	*obsv*
objectionable	*objb*	observer	*Obsv*
objective	*obv*	obsolescence	*obsls/*
objector	*Ob*	obsolescent	*obsls—*
oblate	*oba*	obsolete	*obsle*
oblation	*obj*	obstacle	*obsK*
obligation	*obgj*	obstetric	*obslk*

Word	Shorthand	Word	Shorthand
obstinacy	*(shorthand)*	o'clock	*(shorthand)*
obstinate	*(shorthand)*	octagon	*(shorthand)*
obstreperous	*(shorthand)*	octangular	*(shorthand)*
obstruct	*(shorthand)*	octave	*(shorthand)*
obstruction	*(shorthand)*	October	*(shorthand)*
obstructive	*(shorthand)*	octogenarian	*(shorthand)*
obtain	*(shorthand)*	octopus	*(shorthand)*
obtainable	*(shorthand)*	ocular	*(shorthand)*
obtrude	*(shorthand)*	oculist	*(shorthand)*
obtrusion	*(shorthand)*	odd	*(shorthand)*
obtrusive	*(shorthand)*	oddity	*(shorthand)*
obtuse	*(shorthand)*	oddness	*(shorthand)*
obtuseness	*(shorthand)*	odds	*(shorthand)*
obverse	*(shorthand)*	ode	*(shorthand)*
obviate	*(shorthand)*	odious	*(shorthand)*
obvious	*(shorthand)*	odorous	*(shorthand)*
occasion	*(shorthand)*	odour	*(shorthand)*
occasional	*(shorthand)*	oesophagus	*(shorthand)*
occult	*(shorthand)*	of	*(shorthand)*
occupancy	*(shorthand)*	off	*(shorthand)*
occupant	*(shorthand)*	offal	*(shorthand)*
occupation	*(shorthand)*	offence	*(shorthand)*
occupy	*(shorthand)*	offend	*(shorthand)*
occur	*(shorthand)*	offender	*(shorthand)*
occurrence	*(shorthand)*	offensive	*(shorthand)*
ocean	*(shorthand)*	offer	*(shorthand)*
ocelot	*(shorthand)*	offertory	*(shorthand)*
ochre	*(shorthand)*	office	*(shorthand)*

officer		omen	
official		ominous	
officiate		omission	
officious		omit	
offing		omnibus	
offset		omnipotent	
offspring		omniscience	
often		omniscient	
oftener		omnivorous	
ogle		on	
ogre		once	
oh		one	
ohm		oneness	
oil		onerous	
oilcloth		oneself	
oilskin		onion	
oily		onlooker	
ointment		only	
old		onset	
olden		onslaught	
older		onward	
oleaginous		onyx	
oleander		ooze	
olfactory		opacity	
oligarch		opal	
olive		opalescent	
omega		opaque	
omelet		open	

176

Word	Outline	Word	Outline
openly		optative	
opera		optic	
operate		optical	
operatic		optician	
operation		optimism	
operative		optimist	
operator		option	
operetta		opulent	
ophthalmia		or	
opiate		oracle	
opine		oracular	
opinion		oral	
opinionated		orange	
opium		orangeade	
opponent		oration	
opportune		orator	
opportunism		oratory	
opportunist		orb	
opportunity		orbit	
oppose		orchard	
opposite		orchestra	
opposition		orchid	
oppress		ordain	
oppression		ordeal	
oppressive		order	
oppressor		ordinance	
opprobrious		ordinarily	
opprobrium		ordinary	

English	Shorthand	English	Shorthand
ordination		orthography	
ore		oscillate	
organ		oscillation	
organic		oscillatory	
organism		osculate	
organist		osculatory	
organization		osier	
organize		osprey	
orgasm		osseous	
orgies		ossification	
orient		ossify	
oriental		ostensible	
orifice		ostentation	
origin		ostentatious	
original		osteopathy	
originality		ostler	
originate		ostracism	
origination		ostracize	
originator		ostrich	
ormolu		other	
ornament		otherwise	
ornamental		otter	
ornamentation		ought	
ornate		ounce	
ornithology		our	
orphan		ours	
orphanage		ourselves	
orthodox		oust	

out	*ou*	outreach	
outbalance		outrigger	
outbreak		outright	
outburst		outrun	
outcast		outset	
outcome		outshine	
outcry		outside	
outdoor		outsider	
outer		outskirts	
outermost		outspread	
outfit		outstand	
outfitter		outstretch	
outgrown		outstrip	
outhouse		outvote	
outing		outward	
outlandish		outweigh	
outlast		outwit	
outlaw		outwork	
outlay		oval	
outlet		ovary	
outline		ovation	
outlive		oven	
outlook		over	
outlying		overalls	
outnumber		overawe	
outnumbered		overbalance	
outrage		overbear	
outrageous		overboard	

179

Word	Shorthand	Word	Shorthand
overburden	Vb/n	overpay	Vpa
overcame	Vk	overpower	VP
overcast	Vk,	overprize	Vp3
overcharge	Vcq	overreach	Vrc
overcloud	Vkl_d	override	Vrd
overcoat	Vko	overrule	Vrl
overcome	Vk	overrun	Vrn
overdo	Vdu	oversea	Vse
overdraw	Vda	overseas	Vs3
overdrive	Vdi	overseer	VSe
overdue	Vdu	oversight	Vsi
overestimate	Vesra	overspread	Vsd
overflow	Vflo	overstate	Vsa
overgrow	Vgo	overstep	Vsp
overgrown	Vgn	overstock	Vsk
overhang	Vhq	overstrain	VSn
overhaul	Vhl	overt	ov/
overhead	Vhd	overtake	Vlk
overhear	Vhe	overthrew	Vlu
overjoy	Vjy	overthrow	Vlo
overjoyed	Vjȳ	overtook	Vlk
overlaid	Vld	overture	Vlu
overland	Vl—	overturn	Vln
overlap	Vlp	overweight	V-a
overlay	Vla	overwhelm	V-l
overlook	Vlo	overwork	V-k
overmuch	Vrc	overworked	V-k
overpass	Vp'	oviform	ovf

oviparous	ovpx	ownership	OnЗ
ovoid	ovyd	ox	ox
ovule	ovl	oxen	xn
ovum	ov	oxidate	xda
owe	o	oxide	xd
owl	owl	oxidize	xdз
owlet	owll	oxygen	xɟn
own	on	oyster	yЅ
owner	O^n	ozone	oзn

P

pace	pas	paganism	pgnз
pachyderm	pkdr	page	pɟ
pacific	psfk	pageant	pɟ –
pacification	psf	pageantry	pɟ –,
pacifism	psfз	pagoda	pgda
pacifist	psf,	paid	pd
pacify	psf	pail	pal
pack	pk	pain	pn
package	pkɟ	painful	pnf
packer	Pk	painstaking	pnsk
packet	pkl	paint	pa –
pact	pk	painter	P–
pad	pd	pair (pr)	pa
paddle	pdl	pal	pl
paddock	pdk	palace	pls
padlock	pdlk	palate	pla
pagan	pgn	palatial	plx

181

palatine	*pllun*	pander	*P_*
palaver	*Plv*	pane	*pn*
pale	*pal*	panegyric	*pryrk*
palette	*pll*	panel	*pnl*
palindrome	*pl—o*	pang	*pq*
palisade	*plsd*	panic	*pnk*
pall	*pal*	pannier	*Pn*
palladium	*pld*	panoply	*pnp*
pallbearer	*pl Ba*	panorama	*Pnra*
pallet	*pll*	pansy	*pnz,*
palliate	*pla*	pant	*p-*
palliative	*plv*	pantheism	*pnlz*
palm	*p*	pantheon	*pnln*
palmist	*p,*	panther	*Pn*
palmistry	*pb,*	pantomime	*p- u*
palpable	*plpb*	pantry	*p-,*
palpitate	*plpla*	pap	*pp*
palpitation	*plply*	paper	*Pp.*
palsy	*plz,*	papier-mache	*Ppvza*
paltry	*pll,*	papillary	*pply*
pampas	*prps*	papism	*ppz*
pamper	*Pp*	papist	*pp,*
pamphlet	*pfll*	papyrus	*pprx*
pan	*pn*	par	*pr*
panacea	*prsa*	parable	*Pb*
pancake	*pnkk*	parachute	*Pzu*
pancreas	*pqs*	parade	*prd*
pandemonium	*p— m*	paradise	*Pds*

182

Word	Outline	Word	Outline
paradox	Pdx	parenthetic	prnT
paradoxical	PdxK	parish	P3
paraffin	Pfn	parishioner	Pfr
paragon	Pgn	parity	pr)
paragraph	Pgf	park	prk
parallel	Pll	parlance	prl
parallelogram	Pllg	parley	prl
paralyse	Pl3	parliament	prl –
paralysis	Plss	parliamentary	prl – y
paralytic	Pl7	parlour	Prl
paramount	P⌣ –	parochial	Pkl
paramour	P⌒u	parody	Pd,
parapet	Ppt	parole	prl
paraphernalia	Pfrla	paroxysm	Pxz
paraphrase	Pf3	parricide	Psd
parasite	Pst	parrot	prl
parasol	Psl	parry	pry
parcel	prsl	parse	pr3
parch	prc	parsimonious	prs⌒rx
parchment	prc –	parsimony	prs⌒n,
pardon	p/n	parsley	prsl
pardonable	p/nb	parsnip	prsnp
pare	pa	parson	prsn
paregoric	Pgrk	parsonage	prsny
parent	pr –	part	p/
parentage	pr –|	partake	p/k
parental	pr – l	partaker	P/k
parenthesis	prnlss	partial	prx

183

Word	Shorthand	Word	Shorthand
partiality	prx)	past	P,
participant	p/sp-	paste	pa,
participate	p/spa	pastel	psl
participation	p/spf	pastil	psl
participator	P/spa	pastime	psli
participle	p/sp	pastor	pS
particle	p/K	pastoral	pSl
particular	P/	pastorate	pSa
particularity	P/)	pastry	pS,
particularize	P/3	pasture	psu
partisan	p/3n	pat	pl
partition	P/1	patch	pc
partly	p/l	patent	pl-
partner	P/n	paternal	Parl
partnership	P/nß	paternity	Pan)
partridge	P/1	paternoster	PanS
party	P/,	path	pl
parvenu	prvnu	pathetic	pl⟋
pass	p'	pathological	plolK
passable	psb	pathologist	plol,
passage	psj	pathology	plol
passed	P,	pathos	pls
passenger	Psj	pathway	pl⁀a
passer	p'	patience	pß
passion	Pl	patient	pß-
passionate	pja	patriarch	Paak
passive	psv	patriarchal	Paakl
passivity	psv)	patrician	Paj

184

Word	Shorthand	Word	Shorthand
patricide	Pasd	payer	Pa
patrimonial	Panl	paymaster	pars
patrimony	Pan,	payment	pa-
patriot	Pal	pea	pe
patriotic	PaT	peace	ps
patriotism	Palz	peaceable	psb
patrol	Pal	peaceful	psf
patron	Pan	peacemaker	psUk
patronage	Pary	peach	pec
patroness	Pan'	peacock	pkk
patronize	Panz	peak	pek
patten	plr	peal	pel
patter	Pa	peanut	pnl
pattern	Pan	pear	pa
patty	pl,	pearl	pl
paucity	ps)	peasant	p3-
paunch	pac	peasantry	p3-,
pauper	Pp	peat	pe
pause	p3	pebble	pb
pave	pa	peccadillo	pkdlo
pavement	pa-	peck	pk
pavilion	puln	pectoral	Pkl
paw	pa	peculation	pkly
pawn	pan	peculiar	Pkl
pawnbroker	pnBk	peculiarity	Pkl)
pay	pa	pecuniary	pkny
payable	palb	pedagogue	pdgq
payee	pae	pedal	pdl

185

pedant	pd -	penalty	pnll,
pedantic	pd - k	penance	pn/
pedantry	pd -,	pence	p/
peddler	Pdl	penchant	pc -
pedestal	pdsl	pencil	p/l
pedestrian	pdbn	pendant	p — -
pedigree	pdge	pendency	p —/
pediment	pd -	pendent	p — -
pedlar	Pdl	pending	p —=
pedometer	pdle	pendulous	p —lx
peek	pek	pendulum	p —l
peel	pel	penetrable	pnlb
peep	pep	penetrability	pnlb)
peer	pe	penetrate	pnla
peerage	pey	penetration	pnly
peeress	pe'	penetrative	pnlv
peerless	pel'	penguin	pgn
peevish	pv3	peninsula	p/la
peevishness	pv3'	penitence	pnl/
peg	pq	penitent	pnl -
pelican	plk	penitential	pnlx
pellet	pll	penitentiary	pnlcy
pellucid	plsd	pennant	pn -
pelt	pll	penny	pn,
pelvis	plvs	pension	Pl
pen	pn	pensionary	Ply
penal	pnl	pensioner	Pl
penalize	pnl3	pensive	p/v

186

Word	Outline	Word	Outline
pent	p-	perch	pc
pentagon	p-gn	perchance	pc/
pentameter	p-ʌe	percolate	pkla
penthouse	p-h_s	percolation	pkly
penultimate	pʌllʌa	percolator	Pkla
penumbra	pʌʌba	percussion	pky
penurious	pʌyx	perdition	pdy
penuriousness	pʌyx'	peremptory	pʌy
penury	pʌy	perennial	pʌl
peony	pʌn,	perfect	pfk
people	pp	perfection	pfky
pepper	Pp	perfectly	pfkl
peppermint	Pp-	perfidious	pfdx
pepsin	ppsn	perfidy	pfd,
peptic	ppᴶ	perforate	pfa
per	pʌ	perforation	pfl
peradventure	paʌ-u	perforator	Pfa
perambulate	pʌbla	perforce	pfs
perambulation	pʌby	perform	pf⌐
perambulator	Pʌbla	performance	pf✓
per annum	pa	performer	Pf⌐
perceivable	psʌb	perfume	pfu
perceive	psʌ	perfumer	Pfu
per cent	pc %	perfumery	pfuy
percentage	pcy	perfunctory	pfqy
perceptible	pspb	perhaps	pps
perception	pspy	pericardium	Pk/⌐
perceptive	pspv	pericarp	Pkʌp

187

Word	Shorthand	Word	Shorthand
pericranium	*Phₙₙ*	perpendicular	*Pp — tl*
peril	*Pl*	perpetrate	*ppla*
perilous	*Plx*	perpetration	*ppy*
perimeter	*Pⁿe*	perpetual	*ppll*
period	*Pd*	perpetuate	*pplua*
periodic	*Pdk*	perpetuation	*ppluy*
periodical	*PdK*	perplex	*ppx*
peripatetic	*PpT*	perplexity	*ppx)*
periphery	*Pfy*	perquisite	*pqzl*
periscope	*Pskp*	perry	*py*
perish	*P3*	persecute	*psku*
perishable	*P3b*	persecution	*psky*
perjure	*pju*	persecutor	*Psku*
perjury	*pjy*	perseverance	*psve/*
perk	*pk*	persevere	*psve*
permanency	*pⱽ*	persist	*ps,*
permanent	*pⁿn -*	persistence	*pss/*
permeable	*pⁿb*	person	*psn*
permanganate	*pⁿgra*	personable	*psnb*
permeate	*pⁿa*	personage	*psny*
permissible	*pⁿsb*	personal	*psnl*
permission	*pⁿy*	personality	*psnl)*
permissive	*pⁿsv*	personate	*psna*
permit	*pⁿl*	personification	*psnf/*
permutation	*pⁿuy*	personify	*psnf*
pernicious	*pnx*	perspective	*pskv*
peroration	*Pry*	perspicacious	*pska*
peroxide	*pxd*	perspicacity	*psks)*

188

perspicuity		pest	
perspicuous		pester	
perspiration		pestiferous	
perspire		pestilence	
persuade		pestilent	
persuasion		pestilential	
persuasive		pestle	
persuasiveness		pet	
pert		petal	
pertly		petite	
pertain		petition	
pertinacious		petrel	
pertinacity		petrification	
pertinent		petrify	
perturb		petrol	
perturbation		petroleum	
perusal		petticoat	
peruse		petty	
pervade		petulance	
pervasive		petulant	
perverse		pew	
perversion		pewter	
perversity		phalanx	
pervert		phantasm	
pervious		phantasmagoria	
pessimism		phantom	
pessimist		pharmacist	
pessimistic		pharmacy	

189

phase		photo	
pheasant		photograph	
phenomenal		photographer	
phenomenon		photogravure	
phial		photometer	
philander		phrase	
philanthropical		phraseology	
philanthropist		phrenologist	
philanthropy		phrenology	
philharmonic		phthisis	
philistine		physic	
philologist		physical	
philology		physician	
philosopher		physicist	
philosophic		physics	
philosophical		physiognomy	
philosophize		physiography	
philosophy		physiologist	
phlebotomy		physiology	
phlegm		physique	
phlegmatic		pianist	
phlox		piano	
phoenix		pianoforte	
phone		piastre	
phonetic		piazza	
phosphate		pick	
phosphorescence		pickaxe	
phosphorus		picket	

pickle	pK	pill	pl
picnic	pknk	pillage	plj
pictorial	pkyl	pillar	Pl
picture	pku	pillion	pln
picturesque	pkusk	pillory	ply
pie	pi	pillow	plo
piebald	pibld	pilot	pll
piece	ps	pimento	p-o
piecemeal	ps~l	pimp	p~p
piecework	ps~k	pimpernel	p~pnl
pied	pd	pimple	p~p
pier	pe	pin	pn
pierce	pers	pincers	p//
piety	pi)	pinch	pc
pig	pq	pinchbeck	pcbk
pigeon	pjn	pine	pin
pig iron	pgin	pineapple	pinp
pigment	pq-	pinewood	pin~d
pike	pik	pinion	pnn
pikestaff	pksf	pink	pq
pilaster	plS	pinnace	pns
pilchard	plc/	pinnacle	pnK
pile	pil	pint	pi-
piledriver	pl Di	pioneer	pne
pilfer	plf	pious	pix
pilferage	plfj	pip	pp
pilgrim	plg~	pipe	pip
pilgrimage	plg~j	piper	Pp

Word	Shorthand	Word	Shorthand
pipkin	*ppkn*	pity	*p)*
pippin	*ppn*	pivot	*pvt*
piquancy	*pk/*	placability	*pkb)*
piquant	*pk-*	placable	*pkb*
pique	*pek*	placard	*pk/*
piquet	*pka*	placate	*pka*
piracy	*prs,*	place	*pl*
pirate	*prl*	placement	*pl-*
piratical	*prlk*	placid	*psd*
pirouette	*prul*	placidity	*psd)*
piscatorial	*psklyl*	placidness	*psd'*
pisciculture	*pskllu*	plagiarism	*Pβ*
pistachio	*psβo*	plagiarist	*Pβ,*
pistil	*psl*	plagiarize	*Pβ*
pistol	*psl*	plague	*paq*
piston	*psn*	plaid	*pd*
pit .	*pl*	plain	*pn*
pitch	*pc*	plainer	*Pn*
pitcher	*Pc*	plainly	*pnl*
pitchfork	*pcfk*	plainness	*pn'*
piteous	*plsc*	plaint	*pa-*
pitfall	*plfl*	plaintiff	*p-l*
pith	*pl*	plaintive	*p-v*
pithless	*pll'*	plait	*pl*
pitiable	*plb*	plan	*pn*
pitiful	*plf*	plane	*pn*
pitiless	*pll'*	planet	*pnl*
pittance	*pl/*	planetry	*pnl,*

192

Word	Shorthand	Word	Shorthand
plank	[shorthand]	pleasantness	[shorthand]
plant	[shorthand]	pleasantry	[shorthand]
plantain	[shorthand]	please	[shorthand]
plantation	[shorthand]	pleasure	[shorthand]
planter	[shorthand]	plebeian	[shorthand]
plaque	[shorthand]	plebiscite	[shorthand]
plaster	[shorthand]	pledge	[shorthand]
plastic	[shorthand]	plenary	[shorthand]
plasticity	[shorthand]	plenipotentiary	[shorthand]
plate	[shorthand]	plenitude	[shorthand]
plateau	[shorthand]	plenteous	[shorthand]
platform	[shorthand]	plentiful	[shorthand]
platinum	[shorthand]	plenty	[shorthand]
platitude	[shorthand]	plethora	[shorthand]
platoon	[shorthand]	plethoric	[shorthand]
plaudit	[shorthand]	pleurisy	[shorthand]
plausibility	[shorthand]	plexus	[shorthand]
plausible	[shorthand]	pliability	[shorthand]
play	[shorthand]	pliable	[shorthand]
player	[shorthand]	pliancy	[shorthand]
playfellow	[shorthand]	pliant	[shorthand]
playful	[shorthand]	pliers	[shorthand]
playground	[shorthand]	plight	[shorthand]
playmate	[shorthand]	plinth	[shorthand]
plaything	[shorthand]	plod	[shorthand]
plea	[shorthand]	plot	[shorthand]
plead	[shorthand]	plough	[shorthand]
pleasant	[shorthand]	ploughman	[shorthand]

Word	Outline	Word	Outline
ploughshare		pocketbook	
plover		pod	
pluck		poem	
plucky		poesy	
plug		poet	
plum		poetess	
plumage		poetic	
plumb		poetical	
plumbago		poetry	
plumber		pogrom	
plume		poignancy	
plummet		poignant	
plump		point	
plunder		pointblank	
plunge		pointer	
pluperfect		poise	
plural		poison	
plus		poisonous	
plush		poke	
plutocracy		polar	
plutocrat		polarity	
plutocratic		polarization	
ply		polarize	
pneumatic		pole	
pneumonia		polemic	
poach		police	
pock		policeman	
pocket		policy	

194

polish		polytheism	
polite		polytheist	
politeness		pomade	
politic		pomegranate	
political		pommel	
politician		pomp	
politics		pomposity	
polity		pompous	
polka		pond	
poll		ponder	
pollard		ponderable	
pollen		ponderous	
pollinate		pontiff	
pollute		pontifical	
pollution		pontificate	
polo		pontoon	
polonaise		pony	
polyanthus		poodle	
polygamist		pool	
polygamous		poop	
polygamy		poor	
polyglot		poorer	
polygon		poorly	
polyhedron		pop	
polyp		popcorn	
polypod		Pope	
polysyllable		popery	
polytechnic		popish	

Word	Shorthand	Word	Shorthand
poplar	Pp	porthole	p/hl
poplin	ppn	portico	p/ko
poppy	pp,	portion	pf
populace	ppls	portionless	pfl'
popular	pop	portmanteau	p/⌒-o
popularity	pop)	portrait	p/a
popularize	pop3	portraiture	p/au
popularly	popl	portray	p/a
populate	ppla	pose	p3
population	pplf	position	p3f
populous	pplx	positive	p3v
porcelain	psln	positively	p3vl
porch	pc	positiveness	p3v'
porcupine	pkpin	possess	p3'
pore	po	possession	p3f
pork	pk	possessive	p3sv
porphyry	pfy	possessor	p3'
porpoise	ppx	possibility	psb)
porridge	py	possible	psb
port	p/	post	po,
portable	p/b	postage	py
portage	p/1	postal	psl
portal	p/l	postcard	psk/
portend	p/—	postdiluvian	psdlvn
portentous	p/nx	poster	pS
porter	P/	posterior	pSr
porterage	P/1	posterity	pS)
portfolio	p/flo	posthumous	psnx

postillion	*psln*	pounce	*p*
postman	*psn –*	pound	*lb*
postmark	*psrk*	poundage	*lbj*
postmaster	*psⁿˢ*	pour	*po*
postmeridian	*psrdn*	pout	*pl*
postmortem	*psn√*	poverty	*pv/,*
post-office	*gpo*	powder	*P⌣*
postpone	*psn*	power	*R⌣*
postponement	*psn –*	powerful	*P⌣l*
postcript	*pskp*	powerless	*P⌣l'*
postulant	*psl –*	practicable	*pklb*
postulate	*psla*	practical	*pkK*
posture	*psu*	practice	*pks*
posy	*P3,*	practise	*pks*
pot	*pl*	practitioner	*Pkj*
potash	*plʒ*	pragmatic	*pg√*
potassium	*plsⁿ*	pragmatism	*pglⱬ*
potato	*plto*	pragmatist	*pgl,*
potent	*pl –*	prairie	*Pⱨ*
potentate	*pl – a*	praise	*P3*
potential	*plx*	praiseworthy	*pgrl,*
potentiality	*plx)*	prance	*p*
potion	*Pj*	prank	*pⱪ*
potter	*Pl*	prate	*pa*
pouch	*p⌐*	prattle	*pll*
poulterer	*Pllr*	prawn	*pan*
poultice	*plls*	pray	*pa*
poultry	*pll,*	prayer	*Pa*

prayerful	Paf	precocious	pkx
preach	pec	precocity	pks)
preacher	Pc	precognition	pkgny
preamble	prb	preconceive	pkse
precarious	pkyx	preconception	pkspy
precaution	pky	preconcert	pks/
precautionary	pkyy	precursor	pKrs
precede	psd	predatory	pdly
precedence	psd/	predecease	pdrss
precedent	psd-	predecessor	Pds'
precentor	pS-	predestination	pdsry
precept	psp	predestine	pdsn
preceptor	pSp	predetermination	pDry
preceptress	psp'	predetermine	pDn
precinct	psq	predicable	pdkb
precious	px	predicament	pdk-
precipice	psps	predicate	pdka
precipitance	pspl/	predication	pdky
precipitant	pspl-	predicative	pdkv
precipitate	pspla	predict	pdk
precipitation	psply	predictable	pdkb
precipitous	psplx	prediction	pdky
precise	pss	predictive	pdkv
preciseness	pss'	predilection	pdlky
precision	psy	predispose	pds3
preclude	pkld	predisposition	pds3y
preclusion	pkly	predominance	pd√
preclusive	pklsv	predominant	pdn-

198

predominate	*pd~na*	prelude	*pld*
pre-eminence	*pe~/*	premature	*p~lu*
pre-eminent	*pe~n-*	premeditate	*p~dla*
pre-emption	*pe~y*	premeditation	*p~dly*
preen	*pn*	premier	*P~*
pre-exist	*px,*	premiership	*P~ß*
pre-existence	*pxs/*	premise	*p~s*
preface	*pfs*	premise	*p~z*
prefatory	*pfly*	premium	*p~*
prefect	*pfk*	premonition	*p~ny*
prefecture	*pfku*	premonitory	*p~nly*
prefer	*pl*	preoccupation	*pkpy*
preferable	*pfß*	preoccupy	*pkpu*
preference	*pf*	preordain	*p/n*
preferment	*pl-*	prepaid	*ppd*
prefigure	*pfg*	preparation	*ppay*
prefix	*pfx*	preparative	*pᴾv*
pregnancy	*pg/*	preparatory	*pᴾly*
pregnant	*pgn-*	prepare	*ppa*
prehensile	*ph/l*	prepay	*ppa*
prehistoric	*phŝk*	prepayment	*ppa-*
prejudge	*Py*	preponderance	*pᴾ—/*
prejudice	*pyds*	preponderate	*pᴾ—a*
prejudicial	*pydx*	preposition	*pp3y*
prelate	*pla*	prepositional	*pp3yl*
prelect	*plk*	prepossess	*pp3'*
prelection	*plky*	prepossession	*pp3y*
preliminary	*pl~ny*	preposterous	*ppŝx*

199

Word	Shorthand	Word	Shorthand
prerogative		presumptive	
presage		presumptuous	
presbyter		presuppose	
presbyterian		presupposition	
presbytery		pretend	
prescience		pretence	
prescribe		pretension	
prescription		pretentious	
prescriptive		preternatural	
presence		pretext	
present		prettier	
presentation		prettily	
presented		prettiness	
presently		pretty	
preservation		prevail	
preservative		prevalence	
preserve		prevalent	
preserver		prevaricate	
preside		prevarication	
presidency		prevent	
president		prevention	
presidential		preventive	
press		previous	
pressure		previously	
prestige		prey	
presumably		price	
presume		priceless	
presumption		prick	

200

Word	Outline	Word	Outline
prickle		principality	
prickly		principle	
pride		prink	
priest		print	
priestess		printer	
priesthood		prior	
priestly		prioress	
prig		priority	
priggish		priory	
prim		prise	
prima donna		prism	
primal		prismatic	
primarily		prismatical	
primary		prison	
primacy		prisoner	
primate		pristine	
prime		privacy	
primer		private	
primeval		privateer	
primitive		privation	
primness		privet	
primordial		privilege	
primrose		privily	
prince		privity	
princely		privy	
princess		prize	
principal		probability	
principally		probable	

Word	Shorthand	Word	Shorthand
probably		procurable	
probate		procuration	
probation		procurator	
probationary		procure	
probationer		prodigal	
probatory		prodigality	
probe		prodigious	
probity		prodigy	
problem		produce	
problematic		producible	
problematical		product	
procedure		production	
proceed		productive	
process		productivity	
procession		profane	
proclaim		profanity	
proclamation		profess	
proclivity		profession	
proconsul		professional	
proconsular		professor	
procrastinate		professorial	
procrastination		professorship	
procreate		proffer	
procreation		proficiency	
procreative		proficient	
procreator		profile	
proctor		profit	
procumbent		profitable	

profiteer		prolific	
profitless		prolix	
profligacy		prolixity	
profligate		prologue	
profound		prolong	
profundity		prolongation	
profuse		promenade	
profusion		prominence	
progenitor		prominent	
progeny		promiscuity	
prognostic		promiscuous	
prognosticate		promise	
prognostication		promising	
programme		promissory	
progress		promontory	
progression		promote	
progressive		promotion	
prohibit		prompt	
prohibition		prompter	
prohibitive		promptitude	
prohibitory		promptness	
project		promulgate	
projectile		promulgation	
projection		prone	
projector		prong	
prolate		pronoun	
proletarian		pronounce	
proletariat		pronouncement	

203

pronouncing	ᑭᑎᐧ	proportionate	ᑭᑭᒐ
pronunciation	ᑭᑎᐧ₁	proposal	ᑭᑭᣘ
proof	ᑭᓴ	propose	ᑭᑭᣋ
prop	ᑭᑭ	proposition	ᑭᑭᣋ₁
propaganda	ᑭᑭᓇ — ᵃ	propound	ᑭᑭ‿ —
propagate	ᑭᑭᓇᵃ	proprietary	ᑭᑭᒡᵞ
propagation	ᑭᑭᣋ₁	proprietor	ᑭ_ᒡ
propel	ᑭᑭᔓ	proprietress	ᑭᑭᔓ'
propeller	ᑭ_ᔓ	propriety	ᑭᑭᒡ)
propelling	ᑭᑭᔓ₌	propulsion	ᑭᑭᔓᵞ
propensity	ᑭᑭ')	propulsive	ᑭᑭᔓᣕ
proper	ᑭ_ᑭ	prorogation	ᑭᒡᒡ₁
properly	ᑭᑭᔓ	prorogue	ᑭᒡᒡ
property	ᑭᑭᔓ,	prosaic	ᑭᣘᵏ
prophecy	ᑭᕓᔅ,	proscenium	ᑭᣌᵔ
prophesy	ᑭᕓᣌ	proscribe	ᑭᣌᵏᵇ
prophet	ᑭᕓᔓ	proscription	ᑭᣌᑭᵞ
prophetess	ᑭᕓᔓ'	proscriptive	ᑭᣌᑭᣕ
prophetic	ᑭᕓ	prose	ᑭᣋ
prophetical	ᑭᕓᔓᵏ	prosecute	ᑭᣌᵏᵘ
propinquity	ᑭᑭᣋ)	prosecution	ᑭᣌᵏᵞ
propitiate	ᑭᑭᣍᵃ	prosecutor	ᑭ_ᣌᵏᵘ
propitiation	ᑭᑭᣍ₁	proselyte	ᑭᣌᔓ
propitiatory	ᑭᑭᣍᔓᵞ	prospect	ᑭᣌᵏ
propitious	ᑭᑭᣍᵡ	prospection	ᑭᣌᵏᵞ
proportion	ᑭᑭ₁	prospective	ᑭᣌᵏᣕ
proportionable	ᑭᑭᒐᵇ	prospector	ᑭ_ᣌᵏ
proportional	ᑭᑭᒐᔓ	prospectus	ᑭᣌᵏᵡ

Word	Shorthand	Word	Shorthand
prosper		protrusion	
prosperity		protuberance	
prosperous		protuberant	
prostitute		proud	
prostitution		prouder	
prostrate		prove	
prostration		provender	
protect		proverb	
protection		proverbial	
protective		provide	
protector		providence	
protectorate		provident	
protectorship		providential	
protectress		province	
protege		provincial	
protein		provincialism	
protest		provision	
protestant		provisional	
protestation		proviso	
protocol		provocation	
protoplasm		provocative	
protoplasmic		provoke	
prototype		provost	
protozoa		prow	
protract		prowess	
protraction		prowl	
protractor		proximate	
protrude		proximity	

205

Word	Shorthand	Word	Shorthand
proximo		publisher	
proxy		puce	
prude		pucker	
prudence		pudding	
prudent		puddle	
prudential		puerile	
prudery		puerility	
prudish		puff	
prune		puffin	
prurient		pug	
pry		pugilism	
psalm		pugilist	
psalmist		pugnacious	
psalmody		pugnacity	
pseudonym		puisne	
psychic		puke	
psychological		pule	
psychologist		pull	
psychology		pullet	
ptarmigan		pulley	
puberty		pulmonary	
pubescent		pulp	
public		pulpit	
publican		pulsate	
publication		pulsation	
publicity		pulsative	
publicly		pulsatory	
publish		pulse	

206

pulverize	*Pluʒ*	puppet	*ppl*
puma	*p␣a*	puppy	*pp,*
pumice	*p␣s*	purblind	*pbɪ —*
pummel	*p␣l*	purchasable	*pcsb*
pump	*p␣p*	purchase	*pcs*
pun	*pn*	purchases	*pcss*
punch	*pc*	purchaser	*Pcs*
punctilio	*pqlo*	pure	*pu*
punctilious	*pqlx*	purely	*pul*
punctual	*pql*	purer	*Pu*
punctuality	*pql)*	purgative	*pgv*
punctually	*pql*	purgatory	*pgly*
punctuate	*pqa*	purge	*Pɟ*
punctuation	*pqɟ*	purification	*puf*
puncture	*pqu*	purify	*puf*
pundit	*p—l*	purist	*pu,*
pungency	*Pɟ*	purity	*pu)*
pungent	*Pɟ—*	purl	*pl*
punish	*pnß*	purloin	*plyn*
punishable	*pnßb*	purple	*pp*
punishment	*pnß—*	purport	*pp/*
punitive	*pnv*	purpose	*pps*
punt	*p—*	purposeful	*ppsf*
puny	*pn,*	purposely	*ppsl*
pup	*pp*	purr	*pr*
pupa	*ppa*	purse	*ps*
pupil	*pup*	purser	*Ps*
pupillage	*pupɟ*	pursuance	*psu/*

207

Word	Shorthand	Word	Shorthand
pursuant	ᴘsu –	putative	plʋ
pursue	ᴘsu	putrefaction	plfkɟ
pursuer	Psu	putrefy	plf
pursuit	ᴘsu	putrescence	pls/
purtenance	p/	putrid	pld
purulence	pul/	putt	pl
purulent	pul –	putty	pl,
purvey	pʋa	puzzle	pzl
purveyance	pʋa/	pygmy	pgⁿ,
purveyor	Pʋa	pyjamas	pⁿas
pus	ps	pyramid	Pⁿd
push	pʒ	pyramidal	Pⁿdl
puss	p'	pyrometer	Pⁿe
pustular	Psl	pyrotechnic	Plknk
pustule	psl	pyrotechnical	PlknK
pustulous	pslx	pyrotechnist	Plkn,
put	p	python	pln

Q

Word	Shorthand	Word	Shorthand
quack	qk	quadruped	Qpd
quadrangle	Qɡl	quadruple	Qp
quadrangular	Qɡlr	quadruplicate	Qpka
quadrant	q –	quagmire	qgⁿu
quadrate	Qa	quail	qal
quadratic	Q⫟	quaint	qa –
quadrilateral	Qˌlll	quaintness	q – '
quadrille	Ql	quake	qk
quadroon	Qn	quaker	Qk

208

Word	Outline	Word	Outline
qualification		quench	
qualify		querulous	
qualitative		query	
quality		quest	
qualm		question	
quandary		questionnaire	
quantitative		questionable	
quantity		queue	
quantum		quibble	
quarantine		quick	
quarrel		quicken	
quarrelsome		quickened	
quarry		quicker	
quart		quickest	
quarter		quicklime	
quarterly		quickly	
quartermaster		quickness	
quartet		quicksand	
quarto		quicksilver	
quartz		quiescence	
quash		quiescent	
quasi		quiet	
quaver		quieter	
quay		quietly	
queen		quietness	
queenly		quietude	
queer		quilt	
quell		quince	

Word	Outline	Word	Outline
quinine	*(shorthand)*	quiver	*(shorthand)*
quinsy	*(shorthand)*	quixotic	*(shorthand)*
quintessence	*(shorthand)*	quixotism	*(shorthand)*
quintillion	*(shorthand)*	quiz	*(shorthand)*
quintuple	*(shorthand)*	quoit	*(shorthand)*
quip	*(shorthand)*	quondam	*(shorthand)*
quire	*(shorthand)*	quorum	*(shorthand)*
quirk	*(shorthand)*	quota	*(shorthand)*
quit	*(shorthand)*	quotation	*(shorthand)*
quite	*(shorthand)*	quote	*(shorthand)*
quittance	*(shorthand)*	quotient	*(shorthand)*

R

Word	Outline	Word	Outline
rabbi	*(shorthand)*	racy	*(shorthand)*
rabbinic	*(shorthand)*	radiance	*(shorthand)*
rabbinical	*(shorthand)*	radiant	*(shorthand)*
rabbit	*(shorthand)*	radiate	*(shorthand)*
rabble	*(shorthand)*	radiation	*(shorthand)*
rabid	*(shorthand)*	radiator	*(shorthand)*
rabies	*(shorthand)*	radical	*(shorthand)*
raccoon	*(shorthand)*	radio	*(shorthand)*
race	*(shorthand)*	radioactive	*(shorthand)*
racer	*(shorthand)*	radiograph	*(shorthand)*
racial	*(shorthand)*	radish	*(shorthand)*
raciness	*(shorthand)*	radius	*(shorthand)*
rack	*(shorthand)*	radix	*(shorthand)*
racket	*(shorthand)*	raffle	*(shorthand)*
racoon	*(shorthand)*	raft	*(shorthand)*

210

Word	Shorthand	Word	Shorthand
rafter		rampage	
rag		rampageous	
ragamuffin		rampant	
rage		rampart	
ragged		ramrod	
ragout		ran	
raid		ranch	
rail		rancid	
railing		rancidity	
raillery		rancour	
railway		rancorous	
raiment		random	
rain		rang	
rainbow		range	
raindrop		rank	
rainfall		rankle	
rainy		rankness	
raise		ransack	
raisin		ransom	
rake		rant	
rakish		rap	
rally		rapacious	
ram		rapaciousness	
ramble		rapacity	
rambling		rape	
ramification		rapid	
ramify		rapidity	
ramp		rapidly	

rapier	*Rp*	rationalistic	*ryℓS*
rapt	*rp*	rationality	*ryℓ)*
rapture	*rpu*	rattle	*rℓℓ*
rare	*ra*	rattlesnake	*rℓℓsnk*
rarefaction	*rafky*	ravage	*rvj*
rarefy	*raf*	rave	*ra*
rarely	*raℓ*	ravel	*rvℓ*
rareness	*ra'*	ravelling	*rvℓ_*
rarity	*ra)*	raven	*rvn*
rascal	*rskℓ*	ravenous	*rvnx*
rascality	*rskℓ)*	ravine	*rvn*
rascally	*rskℓ*	ravish	*rvʒ*
rash	*rʒ*	ravishment	*rvʒ-*
rashness	*rʒ'*	raw	*ra*
rasp	*rs*	rawness	*ra'*
raspberry	*rzby*	ray	*ra*
rat	*rℓ*	raze	*rʒ*
ratchet	*rcℓ*	razor	*Rʒ*
rate	*ra*	reach	*rec*
rateable	*rab*	react	*rak*
rather	*Ra*	reaction	*raky*
ratify	*rℓf*	reactionary	*rakyy*
ratification	*rℓf*	read	*rd*
ratio	*rʒo*	read	*rd*
ration	*ry*	reader	*Rd*
rational	*ryℓ*	readier	*Rd,*
rationalism	*ryℓz*	readily	*rdℓ*
rationalist	*ryℓ,*	readiness	*rd'*

212

reading	ᴚd	reassertion	ᴚaᴎ
readjourn	ᴚajᴎ	reassign	ᴚasᴎ
readjust	ᴚaj,	reassignment	ᴚasᴎ –
readmission	ᴚaᴎ	reassume	ᴚasu
readmit	ᴚaᴎ	reassumption	ᴚasᴎ
ready	ᴚd,	reassurance	ᴚaჳu/
reagent	ᴚaj –	reassure	ᴚaჳu
real	ᴚl	rebate	ᴚba
reality	ᴚl)	rebel	ᴚbl
realization	ᴚlᴣ	rebellion	ᴚbln
realize	ᴚlᴣ	rebellious	ᴚblx
really	ᴚl	rebound	ᴚb —
realm	ᴚl⌐	rebuff	ᴚbf
ream	ᴚe	rebuild	ᴚbld
reanimate	ᴚaⁿa	rebuke	ᴚbk
reanimation	ᴚaⁿ	rebut	ᴚbl
reap	ᴚep	rebuttal	ᴚbll
reaper	Rp	recalcitrant	ᴚklsl –
reappear	ᴚap	recall	ᴚkl
reappearance	ᴚap/	recant	ᴚk –
rear	ᴚe	recantation	ᴚk–ᴎ
rearward	ᴚe/	recapitulate	ᴚkplla
reason	ᴚᴣn	recapitulation	ᴚkpllᴣ
reasonable	ᴚᴣnb	recapitulatory	ᴚkpllay
reasonableness	ᴚᴣnb'	recapture	ᴚkpu
reasoning	ᴚᴣn	recast	ᴚk,
reassemble	ᴚasⁿb	recede	ᴚsd
reassert	ᴚas/	receipt	ᴚse

213

English	Shorthand	English	Shorthand
receive		recluse	
receiver		recognition	
recension		recognizance	
recent		recognize	
recently		recoil	
receptacle		recollect	
reception		recollection	
receptive		recommence	
recess		recommencement	
recession		recommend	
recessive		recommendation	
recipe		recommendatory	
recipient		recommit	
reciprocal		recommitment	
reciprocate		recommittal	
reciprocation		recompense	
reciprocity		reconcilable	
recital		reconcile	
recitation		reconcilement	
recitative		reconciliation	
recite		recondite	
reck		reconnaissance	
reckless		reconnoitre	
recklessness		reconsider	
reckon		reconsideration	
reclaim		reconstruct	
reclamation		reconstruction	
recline		record	

recorder	*Rk/*	recuperation	*rkpy*
recount	*rkl*	recuperative	*rkpv*
recoup	*rkp*	recur	*rkr*
recourse	*rkrs*	recurred	*rkr̄*
recover	*rKv*	recurrence	*rkr/*
recovery	*rKv,*	recurrent	*rkr-*
recreate	*rkea*	recurring	*rkr̲*
recreation	*rkey*	recurvature	*rkrvlu*
recreative	*rkev*	recurve	*rkrv*
recriminate	*rk⌢na*	red	*rd*
recrimination	*rk⌢y*	redden	*rdn*
recriminative	*rk⌢nv*	redder	*Rd*
recriminatory	*rk⌢nay*	reddest	*rd,*
recruit	*rku*	reddish	*rdß*
rectangle	*rkagl*	redeem	*rde*
rectangular	*rkAgl*	redeemer	*Rde*
rectification	*rkf/*	redemption	*rdy*
rectify	*rkf*	redirect	*rdrk*
rectilineal	*rklrl*	redness	*rd'*
rectilinear	*rkln*	redolence	*rdl/*
rectitude	*rkld*	redolent	*rdl-*
rector	*Rk*	redouble	*rdb*
rectorial	*rkyl*	redoubt	*rd⌣l*
rectorship	*Rkß*	redoubtable	*rd⌣lb*
rectory	*rky*	redound	*rd—*
rectum	*rk⌢*	redress	*rd'*
recumbent	*rklb-*	reduce	*rds*
recuperate	*rkpa*	reduction	*rdk*

215

redundancy		referee	
redundant		reference	
reduplicate		referendum	
reduplication		refill	
re-echo		refine	
reed		refinement	
reedy		refinery	
reef		refit	
reek		reflect	
reel		reflection	
re-elect		reflective	
re-election		reflector	
re-embark		reflex	
re-embarkation		reflexive	
re-enact		reflux	
re-enactment		reform	
re-enforce		reformation	
re-enforcement		reformative	
re-enter		reformatory	
re-entry		refract	
re-establish		refraction	
re-establishment		refractive	
re-examination		refractory	
re-examine		refrain	
refection		refresh	
refectory		refreshment	
refer		refrigerant	
referable		refrigerate	

216

refrigerator		region	
refuge		register	
refugee		registrar	
refulgence		registration	
refulgent		registry	
refund		regnancy	
refusal		regnant	
refuse		regress	
refuses		regression	
refutation		regressive	
refute		regret	
regain		regretful	
regal		regular	
regale		regularity	
regalia		regulate	
regard		regulation	
regarding		regulative	
regardless		regulator	
regatta		rehabilitate	
regency		rehabilitation	
regenerate		rehearsal	
regeneration		rehearse	
regenerative		reign	
regent		reimburse	
regicide		reimbursement	
regime		rein	
regiment		reindeer	
regimental		reinforce	

reinforcement	*rnfs –*	**release**	*rls*
reinstate	*rnsa*	relegate	*rlga*
reinstatement	*rnsa –*	relegation	*rlg₁*
reintroduce	*rndo*	relent	*rl –*
reintroduction	*rndk₁*	relentless	*rl – l'*
reinvest	*rnv,*	relevance	*rlv*
reinvestment	*rnvs –*	relevancy	*rlv*
reinvigorate	*rnVga*	relevant	*rlv –*
reinvigoration	*rnVg₁*	reliability	*rlib)*
reissue	*rużu*	reliable	*rlib*
reiterate	*rȝa*	reliance	*rli*
reiteration	*rȝ₁*	reliant	*rli –*
reject	*ryk*	relic	*rlk*
rejection	*ryk₁*	relief	*rlf*
rejoice	*ryys*	relieve	*rle*
rejoicing	*ryys̲*	religion	*rlyn*
rejoin	*ryyn*	religious	*rlyx*
rejoinder	*ryy —*	religiousness	*rlyx'*
rejuvenate	*ryvna*	relinquish	*rlqß*
rekindle	*rk — l*	relish	*rlß*
relapse	*rlps*	reluctance	*rlk/*
relate	*rla*	reluctant	*rlk –*
relation	*rl₁*	reluctantly	*rlk – l*
relationship	*rlß*	rely	*rli*
relative	*rlv*	remain	*rn*
relax	*rlx*	remainder	*Rn*
relaxation	*rlx₁*	remand	*rn —*
relay	*rla*	remark	*rrk*

218

Word	Shorthand	Word	Shorthand
remarkable		remover	
remediable		remunerate	
remedial		remuneration	
remedy		remunerative	
remember		renascent	
remembrance		renal	
remind		rend	
reminder		render	
reminiscence		rendition	
remiss		rendezvous	
remission		renegade	
remissness		renew	
remit		renewable	
remittance		renewal	
remnant		rennet	
remodel		renounce	
remonstrance		renouncement	
remonstrate		renovate	
remorse		renovation	
remorseful		renown	
remorsefulness		rent	
remorseless		rental	
remote		renunciation	
remoteness		reopen	
remount		reorganization	
removable		reorganize	
removal		repaid	
remove		repair	

Word	Outline	Word	Outline
repairer	Rpa	replica	rpka
reparable	rPb	reply	rpu
reparation	rf	report	rp/
repartee	rp/e	reporter	Rp/
repast	rp,	repose	rp3
repatriate	rPaa	repository	rpzly
repatriation	rPay	repossess	rp3'
repay	rpa	repossession	rp31
repayment	rpa -	reprehend	rph —
repeal	rpl	reprehensible	rph/b
repeat	rpe	reprehension	rphy
repeatedly	rpe l.	reprehensive	rph/v
repel	rpl	represent	rep
repellent	rpl -	representation	rep1
repent	rp -	representative	rep
repentance	rp /	repress	rp'
repentant	rp - -	repression	rp1
repercussion	rpk1	repressive	rpsv
repertoire	rpl a	reprieve	rpe
repertory	rply	reprimand	rp ⌢ —
repetition	rp1y	reprint	rp -
repine	rpun	reprisal	rpzl
replace	rpl	reproach	rpc
replacement	rpl -	reproachful	rpcf
replenish	rpn3	reprobate	rpba
replenishment	rpn3 -	reprobation	rpb1
replete	rpe	reproduce	rpds
repletion	rp1	reproduction	rpdky

reproductive	_rpdkv_	requite	_rqt_
reproof	_rpf_	rescind	_rs —_
reprovable	_rpvb_	rescue	_rsku_
reprove	_rpv_	research	_rsc_
reptile	_rpl_	resemblance	_rz b_
republic	_rpb_	resemble	_rz b_
republican	_rpbn_	resent	_rz -_
republicanism	_rpbnz_	resentful	_rz - f_
republication	_rpbj_	resentment	_rz - -_
republish	_rpb_	reservation	_rsvj_
repudiate	_rpda_	reserve	_rsv_
repudiation	_rpdj_	reservoir	_rsv a_
repugnance	_rpg/_	reset	_rsl_
repugnant	_rpgn -_	reside	_rzd_
repulse	_rpls_	residence	_rzd/_
repulsion	_rplj_	residency	_rzd/_
repulsive	_rplsv_	resident	_rzd -_
repurchase	_rpcs_	residential	_rzdsc_
reputable	_rpub_	residentiary	_rzdcy_
reputation	_rpuj_	residual	_rzdl_
repute	_rpu_	residuary	_rzdy_
request	_rq,_	residue	_rzdu_
requiem	_rq_	resign	_rzin_
require	_rqt_	resignation	_rzgrj_
requirement	_rqt -_	resiliency	_rzl/_
requisite	_rqzl_	resilient	_rzl -_
requisition	_rqzj_	resin	_rzn_
requital	_rqll_	resinous	_rznx_

Word	Shorthand	Word	Shorthand
resist		responsible	
resistance		responsive	
resistible		rest	
resolute		restaurant	
resolution		restaurateur	
resolve		restful	
resonance		restfulness	
resonant		restitution	
resort		restive	
resound		restless	
resource		restlessness	
resourceful		restoration	
resources		restorative	
respect		restore	
respectability		restorer	
respectable		restrain	
respectful		restraint	
respective		restrict	
respiration		restrictive	
respirator		result	
respiratory		resultant	
respire		resume	
respite		resumption	
resplendence		resurgence	
resplendent		resurgent	
respond		resurrection	
response		resuscitate	
responsibility		resuscitation	

222

Word	Outline	Word	Outline
retail	*(shorthand)*	retrogression	*(shorthand)*
retain	*(shorthand)*	retrogressive	*(shorthand)*
retainer	*(shorthand)*	retrospect	*(shorthand)*
retaliate	*(shorthand)*	retrospection	*(shorthand)*
retaliation	*(shorthand)*	retrospective	*(shorthand)*
retaliatory	*(shorthand)*	return	*(shorthand)*
retard	*(shorthand)*	reunion	*(shorthand)*
retardation	*(shorthand)*	reunite	*(shorthand)*
retch	*(shorthand)*	reveal	*(shorthand)*
retention	*(shorthand)*	revel	*(shorthand)*
retentive	*(shorthand)*	revelation	*(shorthand)*
reticence	*(shorthand)*	revelry	*(shorthand)*
reticent	*(shorthand)*	revenge	*(shorthand)*
retina	*(shorthand)*	revengeful	*(shorthand)*
retinue	*(shorthand)*	revenue	*(shorthand)*
retire	*(shorthand)*	reverberate	*(shorthand)*
retirement	*(shorthand)*	reverberation	*(shorthand)*
retort	*(shorthand)*	revere	*(shorthand)*
retouch	*(shorthand)*	reverence	*(shorthand)*
retrace	*(shorthand)*	reverend	*(shorthand)*
retract	*(shorthand)*	reverent	*(shorthand)*
retractile	*(shorthand)*	reverential	*(shorthand)*
retreat	*(shorthand)*	reverie	*(shorthand)*
retribution	*(shorthand)*	reversal	*(shorthand)*
retributive	*(shorthand)*	reverse	*(shorthand)*
retrieve	*(shorthand)*	reversible	*(shorthand)*
retrocession	*(shorthand)*	reversion	*(shorthand)*
retrograde	*(shorthand)*	reversionary	*(shorthand)*

Word	Shorthand	Word	Shorthand
revert		rheumatism	
review		rhinoceros	
revile		rhododendron	
revise		rhubarb	
revision		rhyme	
revisit		rhymer	
revival		rhymester	
revivalism		rhythm	
revivalist		rhythmic	
revive		rhythmical	
revocable		rib	
revocation		ribald	
revoke		ribaldry	
revolt		ribband	
revolting		ribbon	
revolution		rice	
revolutionary		rich	
revolutionize		richer	
revolve		riches	
revolver		richly	
revulsion		richness	
reward		rick	
rhapsody		rickets	
rheostat		rickety	
rhetoric		rickshaw	
rhetorical		ricochet	
rheum		rid	
rheumatic		riddance	

224

ridden	ɹdn	ring	ɹq
riddle	ɹdl	ringer	Rq
ride	ɹd	ringleader	ɹqld
rider	Rd	ringworm	ɹqɯ~
ridge	ɹy	rinse	ɹ/
ridicule	ɹdkl	riot	ɹul
ridicule ✓	ɹdklx	riotous	ɹulx
riding	ɹd̲	rip	ɹp
rife	ɹɥ	riparian	ɹpyn
rifle	ɹfl	ripe	ɹup
rifleman	ɹfl~ -	ripen	ɹpn
rift	ɹɥ	ripeness	ɹp'
rig	ɹq	ripple	ɹp
right	ɹu	rise	ɹʒ
righteous	ɹux	risen	ɹʒn
righteousness	ɹux'	risibility	ɹʒb)
rightful	ɹɥ	risible	ɹʒb
rightly	ɹul	risk	ɹsk
rigid ✓	ɹyd	rite	ɹu
rigidity	ɹyd)	ritual	ɹll
rigmarole	ɹgɯɹl	ritualistic	ɹllS
rigour	Rq	rival	ɹvl
rigorous	Rgx	rivalled	ɹvl̄
rile	ɹul	rivalry	ɹvl,
rim	ɹ⌒	rive	ɹu
rime	ɹu	riven	ɹun
rind	ɹu —	river	Rv
rinderpest	R— p,	riverside	Rvsd

Word	Outline	Word	Outline
rivet		rodomontade	
rivulet		roe	
roach		roebuck	
road		rogation	
roadside		rogue	
roadstead		roguery	
roadster		roguish	
roadway		roister	
roam		role	
roan		roll	
roar		roller	
roast		rollick	
roaster		romance	
rob		romantic	
robber		romanticism	
robbery		romp	
robe		romper	
robin		rompish	
robust		rondeau	
rochet		rood	
rock		roof	
rocker		roofing	
rockery		roofless	
rocket		rook	
rocky		rookery	
rod		room	
rode		roominess	
rodent		roomy	

roost	ru,	rotundity	rl —)
rooster	rus	rouble	rb
root	ru	rouge	ruy
rootlet	rull	rough	rf
rope	rop	roughen	rfn
ropery	rpy	roulette	rll
ropiness	rp'	round	r ——
rosaceous	rzx	rounder	R ——
rosary	rzy	roundly	r —l
rose	rz	roundness	r —'
roseate	rza	rouse	r3
rosebud	rzbd	rout	rl
rosemary	rzy	route	ru
rosette	rzl	routine	rln
rosewood	rzd	rove	ro
rosin	rzn	rover	Ro
rostrum	rs	row	ro
rosy	rz,	row	r
rot	rl	rowan	rn
rotary	rly	rowdy	rd,
rotate	rla	rowdyism	rdz
rotation	rly	rowel	rl
rotatory	rlay	rowlock	rlk
rote	ro	royal	ryl
rotten	rln	royalist	ryl,
rottenness	rln'	royalty	ryll,
rotund	rl ——	rub	rb
rotunda	rl — a	rubber	Rb

227

rubbish		ruminate	
rubble		rumination	
rubicund		rummage	
rubric		rumour	
ruby		rump	
rudder		rumple	
ruddy		run	
rude		runabout	
rudeness		runaway	
rudiment		rung	
rudimental		runner	
rudimentary		runt	
rue		rupee	
rueful		rupture	
ruff		rural	
ruffian		ruralize	
ruffianly		ruse	
ruffle		rush	
rug		rushing	
rugged		rusk	
ruggedness		russet	
ruin		rust	
ruinous		rustic	
rule		rusticate	
ruler		rustle	
rum		rusty	
rumble		rut	
ruminant		ruthless	

228

rye	ᴗ		

S

sabbath		sadden	
sabre		sadder	
sable		saddle	
sabot		saddler	
sabotage		saddlery	
sac		sadness	
saccharine		safe	
sacerdotal		safeguard	
sachet		safely	
sack		safer	
sackcloth		safety	
sacrament		safety-valve	
sacramental		saffron	
sacred		sag	
sacredness		saga	
sacrifice		sagacious	
sacrificial		sagacity	
sacrificially		sage	
sacrilege		sagely	
sacrilegious		sago	
sacrilegiously		said	
sacrist		sail	
sacristan		sailor	
sacristy		saint	
sad		saintlike	

229

saintly		salvation	
sake		salve	
salaam		salver	
salacious		salvo	
salad		same	
salamander		sameness	
salary		sample	
sale		sampler	
saleable		sanatorium	
salesman		sanatory	
salient		sanctification	
saline		sanctify	
saliva		sanctimonious	
salivary		sanctimoniousness	
sallow		sanctimony	
sallowness		sanction	
sally		sanctity	
salmon		sanctuary	
saloon		sanctum	
salt		sand	
saltiness		sandal	
salubrious		sandalwood	
salubrity		sandman	
salutary		sandpiper	
salutation		sandwich	
salutatory		sandy	
salute		sane	
salvage		saneness	

sang	~q	satellite	ált
sang-froid	~gf—a	satiable	~ßb
sanguinary	~gry	satiate	~ßa
sanguine	~gn	satiety	~lt)
sanitary	~nly	satin	~ln
sanitation	~nly	satinwood	~ln—d
sanity	~n)	satire	~lt
sank	~q,	satiric	~brk
sap	~p	satirical	~brK
sapid	~pd	satirically	~brK
sapidity	~pd)	satirist	~br,
sapience	~p/ :	satirize	~brz
sapient	~p -	satisfaction	~sal
sapless	~pl '	satisfactory	~sal
sapling	~pq	satisfy	~sal
sapphire	~fr	saturate	~lua
sappy	~p,	saturation	~luy
sarcasm	~rkz	Saturday	~l
sarcastic	~rkS	saturnalia	~lnla
sarcastically	~rksK	saturnine	~lnun
sarcophagus	~rkfgx	satyr	la
sardine	s/n	sauce	~sas
sardonic	s/nk	saucepan	~sspn
sartorial	s/yl	saucer	ls
sash	~ß	sauciness	~ss '
sat	~l	saucy	~ss,
satchel	~cl	saunter	l-
sateen	~len	sausage	~ssy

231

Word	Outline	Word	Outline
savage		scamper	
savagery		scan	
savanna		scandal	
save		scandalize	
saveloy		scandalous	
saver		scant	
saving		scantiness	
saviour		scantling	
savour		scanty	
savoury		scape	
saw		scapegoat	
sawdust		scapegrace	
sawmill		scapular	
sawyer		scar	
saxifrage		scarab	
saxophone		scarce	
say		scarcely	
scab		scarceness	
scabbard		scarcity	
scaffold		scare	
scaffolding		scarecrow	
scald		scarf	
scale		scarification	
scallop		scarify	
scalp		scarlet	
scalpel		scathe	
scaly		scatheless	
scamp		scathing	

232

Word	Shorthand	Word	Shorthand
scatter		sciatica	
scavenger		science	
scenario		scientific	
scene		scientist	
scenery		scimitar	
scenic		scintilla	
scent		scintillate	
sceptic		scintillation	
sceptical		scion	
scepticism		scissors	
sceptre		scoff	
schedule		scoffer	
scheme		scoffingly	
scheming		scold	
schism		scoop	
schismatic		scope	
schismatical		scorbutic	
scholar		scorch	
scholarly		score	
scholarship		scorn	
scholastic		scorner	
school		scornful	
schoolboy		scorpion	
schoolhouse		scotch	
schoolmaster		Scotland	
schoolroom		Scots	
schooner		Scottish	
sciatic		scoundrel	

Word	Outline	Word	Outline
scour	sk	scroll	skol
scourge	skrg	scrub	skb
scout	skt	scruple	skp
scowl	skl	scrupulous	skplx
scrag	skq	scrutineer	sklne
scraggy	skq,	scrutinize	sklnz
scramble	sk-b	scrutiny	skln,
scrap	skp	scud	skd
scrape	skap	scuffle	skfl
scraper	Skp	scull	skl
scratch	skc	scullery	skly
scrawl	skal	scullion	skln
scream	ske	sculptor	Sklp
screech	skec	sculpture	sklpu
screen	skn	scum	sk
screw	sku	scupper	Skp
scribble	skb	scurf	skrf
scribe	skib	scurrile	skrl
scrim	sk	scurrility	skrl)
scrimmage	skrg	scurrilous	skrlx
scrimp	sk-p	scurrilousness	skrlx'
scrip	skp	scurry	sky
script	skpl	scurvily	skrvl
scriptural	skpul	scurvy	skrv,
scripture	skpu	scuttle	skll
scrivener	Skvn	scythe	sl
scrofula	skfla	sea	se
scrofulous	skflx	seacoast	sek,

234

Word	Outline	Word	Outline
seafarer	*(shorthand)*	secretariat	*(shorthand)*
seafaring	*(shorthand)*	secretary	*(shorthand)*
seal	*(shorthand)*	sect	*(shorthand)*
seam	*(shorthand)*	section	*(shorthand)*
seamen	*(shorthand)*	sector	*(shorthand)*
seance	*(shorthand)*	secure	*(shorthand)*
seaport	*(shorthand)*	security	*(shorthand)*
sear	*(shorthand)*	sedan	*(shorthand)*
search	*(shorthand)*	sedate	*(shorthand)*
seashore	*(shorthand)*	sedateness	*(shorthand)*
seasick	*(shorthand)*	sedative	*(shorthand)*
seaside	*(shorthand)*	sedentary	*(shorthand)*
season	*(shorthand)*	sedge	*(shorthand)*
seasonable	*(shorthand)*	sediment	*(shorthand)*
seasoning	*(shorthand)*	sedimentary	*(shorthand)*
seat	*(shorthand)*	sedition	*(shorthand)*
seaward	*(shorthand)*	seditious	*(shorthand)*
seaway	*(shorthand)*	seduce	*(shorthand)*
sebaceous	*(shorthand)*	seduction	*(shorthand)*
secede	*(shorthand)*	seductive	*(shorthand)*
secession	*(shorthand)*	sedulous	*(shorthand)*
seclude	*(shorthand)*	see	*(shorthand)*
seclusion	*(shorthand)*	seed	*(shorthand)*
second	*(shorthand)*	seedling	*(shorthand)*
secondary	*(shorthand)*	seedsman	*(shorthand)*
secrecy	*(shorthand)*	seedtime	*(shorthand)*
secret	*(shorthand)*	seeing	*(shorthand)*
secretarial	*(shorthand)*	seek	*(shorthand)*

Word	Outline	Word	Outline
seeker		selves	
seem		semaphore	
seemingly		semblance	
seemliness		semester	
seemly		semibreve	
seen		semicircle	
seer		semicircular	
seesaw		semicolon	
seethe		semiconscious	
segment		seminal	
segregate		seminary	
segregation		semiquaver	
seismic		semitone	
seismograph		semitransparent	
seismometer		semolina	
seize		sempstress	
seizure		senate	
seldom		senator	
select		senatorial	
selection		send	
self		sender	
selfish		senile	
selfishness		senility	
selfless		senior	
selfsame		seniority	
sell		senna	
seller		sensation	
selvedge		sensational	

sense		separator	
senseless		sepia	
sensibility		September	
sensible		septennial	
sensibly		septic	
sensitive		septuagenarian	
sensorial		sepulchral	
sensory		sepulchre	
sensual		sequel	
sensualist		sequence	
sensuality		sequester	
sensuous		sequestrate	
sent		sequestration	
sentence		sequestrator	
sentential		sequin	
sententious		seraph	
sentient		seraphim	
sentiment		serenade	
sentimental		serene	
sentimentalist		sereness	
sentimentality		serenity	
sentinel		serf	
sentry		serge	
separable		sergeant	
separate		serial	
separately		series	
separation		serious	
separatist		seriously	

237

D.—Q

Word	Outline	Word	Outline
seriousness		seventeenth	
sermon		seventh	
sermonize		seventy	
serpent		sever	
serpentine		several	
serrate		severally	
serried		severance	
serum		severe	
servant		severity	
serve		severeness	
server		sew	
service		sewage	
serviceable		sewer	
servile		sewerage	
servility		sex	
servitor		sexagenarian	
servitude		sextant	
sesame		sexton	
session		sextuple	
set		sexual	
settee		shabbily	
setter		shabbiness	
settle		shabby	
settlement		shackle	
settler		shade	
seven		shadow	
sevenfold		shadowy	
seventeen		shady	

238

shaft	shark
shagginess	sharp
shaggy	sharpen
shah	sharpener
shake	sharper
shaker	sharpness
shall	sharpshooter
shallot	shatter
shallow	shave
shallowness	shaven
sham	shaver
shamble	shaving
shame	shawl
shameful	she
shamefulness	sheaf
shameless	shear
shamelessness	sheathe
shammy	sheaves
shampoo	shed
shamrock	sheen
shank	sheep
shan't	sheepishness
shanty	sheepshearing
shape	sheer
shapeless	sheet
shapely	sheik
share	shekel
shareholder	shelf

Word	Shorthand	Word	Shorthand
shell		shirt	
shellac		shiver	
shelter		shoal	
shelve		shock	
shepherd		shod	
shepherdess		shoddy	
sherbet		shoe	
sheriff		shoemaker	
sherry		shoes	
shield		shone	
shift		shook	
shifting		shoot	
shiftless		shooter	
shiftlessness		shop	
shillelagh		shopkeeper	
shilling		shoplifter	
shimmer		shopper	
shin		shopwalker	
shine		shore	
shingle		shorn	
shining		short	
ship		shortage	
shipment		shorten	
shipper		shorter	
shipwreck		shorthand	
shipyard		shortly	
shire		shot	
shirk		shotgun	

Word	Shorthand	Word	Shorthand
should		shuffle	
shoulder		shun	
shout		shunt	
shove		shut	
shovel		shutter	
show		shuttle	
shower		shy	
showery		sibilant	
shrank		sick	
shrapnel		sicken	
shred		sickle	
shrewd		sickly	
shrewish		sickness	
shriek		side	
shrill		sideboard	
shrillness		sidelong	
shrimp		sidereal	
shrine		sideways	
shrink		siege	
shrivel		sienna	
shrivelling		sierra	
shroud		siesta	
shrub		sieve	
shrubbery		sift	
shrubby		sigh	
shrug		sight	
shrunk		sightless	
shudder		sightly	

Word	Shorthand	Word	Shorthand
sign	*(shorthand)*	simile	*(shorthand)*
signal	*(shorthand)*	similitude	*(shorthand)*
signalize	*(shorthand)*	simmer	*(shorthand)*
signalling	*(shorthand)*	simper	*(shorthand)*
signatory	*(shorthand)*	simple	*(shorthand)*
signature	*(shorthand)*	simpleton	*(shorthand)*
signet	*(shorthand)*	simplicity	*(shorthand)*
significance	*(shorthand)*	simplification	*(shorthand)*
significant	*(shorthand)*	simplify	*(shorthand)*
signification	*(shorthand)*	simply	*(shorthand)*
signify	*(shorthand)*	simulate	*(shorthand)*
silence	*(shorthand)*	simulation	*(shorthand)*
silent	*(shorthand)*	simulator	*(shorthand)*
silhouette	*(shorthand)*	simultaneous	*(shorthand)*
silica	*(shorthand)*	sin	*(shorthand)*
silk	*(shorthand)*	since	*(shorthand)*
silken	*(shorthand)*	sincere	*(shorthand)*
silkworm	*(shorthand)*	sincerity	*(shorthand)*
sill	*(shorthand)*	sinecure	*(shorthand)*
silliness	*(shorthand)*	sinecurist	*(shorthand)*
silly	*(shorthand)*	sinew	*(shorthand)*
silo	*(shorthand)*	sinewy	*(shorthand)*
silt	*(shorthand)*	sinful	*(shorthand)*
silver	*(shorthand)*	sinfulness	*(shorthand)*
silverware	*(shorthand)*	sing	*(shorthand)*
silvery	*(shorthand)*	singe	*(shorthand)*
similar	*(shorthand)*	singer	*(shorthand)*
similarity	*(shorthand)*	single	*(shorthand)*

singly	sgl	sixteen	16
singular	Sgl	sixteenth	16L
singularity	Sgl)	sixth	6L
sinister	snS	sixthly	6l
sink	sq	sixty	60
sinless	snl'	sizar	Sz
sinner	Sn	size	sz
sinning	sn	skate	ska
sinuosity	snus)	skein	skn
sinuous	snux	skeleton	sklln
sinus	sinx	sketch	skc
sip	sp	skew	sku
siphon	sfn	skewer	Sku
sir	sr	ski	ske
sire	su	skid	skd
siren	srn	skies	skz
sirloin	slyn	skiff	skf
sirocco	srko	skilful	skll
sister	sS	skill	skl
sisterhood	sShd	skim	sk
sisterly	sSl	skin	skn
sit	sl	skinny	skn,
site	su	skins	skns
situate	sla	skip	skp
situation	sul	skipper	Skp
six	6	skirmish	skr~ß
sixfold	6fol	skirt	sk/
sixpence	6p	skit	skl

Word	Shorthand	Word	Shorthand
skittish	*sklʒ*	slatternly	*slnl*
skittles	*sklls*	slaughter	*sa*
skulk	*sklk*	slave	*sa*
skull	*skl*	slavery	*say*
skunk	*skq*	slavish	*saʒ*
sky	*ski*	slay	*sa*
skyblue	*skibu*	slayer	*sa*
skylark	*skilrk*	sled	*sd*
skylight	*skili*	sledge	*sy*
skyscraper	*skiskp*	sleek	*sek*
skyward	*ski/*	sleep	*sep*
slab	*sb*	sleeper	*sp*
slack	*sk*	sleepiness	*sp'*
slacken	*skn*	sleepless	*spl'*
slackness	*sk'*	sleeplessness	*sp"*
slag	*sq*	sleepy	*sp,*
slain	*sn*	sleet	*se*
slake	*sk*	sleeve	*se*
slam	*sn*	sleeveless	*sel'*
slander	*s—*	sleigh	*sa*
slanderous	*s—x*	sleight	*su*
slang	*sq*	slender	*s—*
slant	*s-*	slenderness	*s—'*
slap	*sp*	slept	*sp*
slash	*sʒ*	slew	*su*
slat	*sl*	slice	*sus*
slate	*sa*	slid	*sd*
slattern	*sln*	slide	*sd*

244

Word	Outline	Word	Outline
slight		slowness	
slim		slug	
slime		sluggard	
slimy		sluggish	
sling		sluggishly	
slink		sluggishness	
slip		sluice	
slipper		slum	
slippery		slumber	
slipshod		slumberous	
slit		slump	
slobber		slung	
sloe		slunk	
slog		slur	
slogan		slush	
sloop		slut	
slop		sly	
slope		slyly	
slot		slyness	
sloth		smack	
slothful		small	
slothfulness		smaller	
slouch		smart	
slough		smartness	
sloven		smash	
slovenliness		smatter	
slow		smatterer	
slower		smattering	

smear		snapdragon	
smell		snare	
smelt		snarl	
smile		snatch	
smilingly		sneak	
smirch		sneer	
smirk		sneeze	
smite		sniff	
smith		snip	
smithy		snipe	
smitten		snivel	
smock		snivelling	
smoke		snob	
smoker		snobbery	
smooth		snobbish	
smoothness		snood	
smote		snooze	
smother		snore	
smoulder		snort	
smug		snout	
smuggle		snow	
smut		snowball	
smutty		snowdrop	
snack		snowflake	
snag		snowy	
snail		snub	
snake		snuff	
snap		snuffle	

246

Word	Shorthand	Word	Shorthand
snug		soft	
so		soften	
soak		softer	
soap		softly	
soapsuds		softness	
soar		soil	
sob		soiree	
sobbing		sojourn	
sober		sojourner	
soberness		solace	
sobriety		solar	
sobriquet		sold	
sociability		solder	
sociable		soldier	
sociably		soldierlike	
social		soldiery	
socially		sole	
socialist		solecism	
socialistic		solemn	
socialize		solemnity	
society		solemnize	
sock		sol-fa	
socket		solicit	
sod		solicitation	
soda		solicitor	
sodality		solicitous	
sodden		solicitude	
sofa		solid	

247

Word	Shorthand	Word	Shorthand
solidarity		sometime	
solidification		somewhat	
solidify		somewhere	
solidity		somnambulism	
soliloquize		somnambulist	
soliloquy		somnolence	
solitaire		somnolent	
solitary		son	
solitude		sonata	
solo		song	
soloist		songster	
solstice		songstress	
solubility		sonnet	
soluble		sonorous	
solution		soon	
solve		soot	
solvable		sooth	
solvency		sooty	
solvent		sop	
sombre		sophism	
sombrely		sophist	
sombreness		sophistical	
some		sophisticate	
somebody		sophistication	
somehow		sophistry	
someone		sophomore	
somersault		soporiferous	
something		soporific	

Word	Shorthand	Word	Shorthand
soprano		south	
sorcerer		southeast	
sorceress		southeastern	
sorcery		southerly	
sordid		southern	
sordidness		southernmost	
sore		southward	
soreness		southwest	
sorority		southwestern	
sorrel		souvenir	
sorrow		sovereign	
sorrowful		sovereignty	
sorry		sow	
sort		sow	
sorter		space	
sortie		spacious	
sot		spade	
sought		spaghetti	
soul		span	
soulless		spandrel	
sound		spangle	
sounder		spaniel	
soundness		spank	
soup		spar	
sour		spare	
source		spark	
sourness		sparkle	
souse		sparrow	

249

Word	Outline	Word	Outline
sparse		spectator	
sparsely		spectral	
sparsity		spectre	
spasm		spectroscope	
spasmodic		spectrum	
spasmodical		specula	
spat		specular	
spate		speculate	
spatter		speculation	
spawn		speculative	
speak		speculator	
speaker		sped	
spear		speech	
spearmint		speechless	
special		speechlessness	
specialist		speed	
specialization		speedometer	
specialty		Speedtyping	
species		Speedwriter	
specific		Speedwriting	
specification		speedy	
specify		spell	
specimen		spellbound	
specious		spelt	
speck		spend	
speckle		spender	
spectacle		spendthrift	
spectacular		spent	

Word	Outline	Word	Outline
sperm		spiritualism	
spew		spiritualist	
sphere		spirituality	
spherical		spirituous	
spheroid		spit	
sphinx		spite	
spice		spiteful	
spicery		spitefulness	
spicy		splash	
spider		splay	
spike		spleen	
spiky		splendid	
spill		splendour	
spilt		splenetic	
spin		splice	
spinach		splint	
spinal		splinter	
spindle		split	
spine		splitting	
spinet		splutter	
spinster		spoil	
spiny		spoke	
spinney		spoken	
spiral		spokesman	
spire		spoliation	
spirit		sponge	
spiritless		spongy	
spiritual		sponsor	

Word	Shorthand	Word	Shorthand
spontaneity	s–n)	springtime	ɀgu
spontaneous	s–nx	sprinkle	ɀql
spool	sul	sprint	ɀ–
spoon	sn	sprite	ɀu
spoonful	snf	sprout	ɀl
spoor	su	spruce	ɀus
sporadic	srdk	sprung	ɀq
spore	so	spry	ɀu
sporran	srn	spume	su
sport	s/	spun	sn
sportive	s/v	spunk	sq
sportsman	s//⌒–	spur	sr
spot	sl	spurious	syx
spotless	sll'	spurn	srn
spouse	s3	spurring	sr
spout	sl	spurt	s/
sprain	ɀn	sputter	Su
sprang	ɀq	spy	su
sprat	ɀl	squab	sqb
sprawl	ɀol	squabble	sqb
spray	ɀa	squad	sqd
spread	ɀd	squadron	sqdn
spreader	5d	squalid	sqld
spree	ɀe	squall	sqal
sprig	ɀq	squally	sqf,
sprightly	ɀul	squalor	sqf
spring	ɀq	squander	sq—
springtide	ɀgld	square	sq

252

Word	Shorthand	Word	Shorthand
squarely		staid	
squash		stain	
squat		stainless	
squaw		stair	
squeak		staircase	
squeal		stairway	
squeamish		stake	
squeeze		stalactite	
squeezer		stalagmite	
squib		stale	
squint		staleness	
squire		stalk	
squirrel		stall	
squirt		stallion	
stab		stalwart	
stability		stamen	
stable		stamina	
stabling		stammer	
staccato		stamp	
stack		stampede	
stadium		stance	
staff		stanch	
stag		stanchion	
stage		stand	
stagger		standard	
stagnant		standing	
stagnate		stank	
stagnation		stanza	

253

staple		station	
stapler		stationary	
star		stationer	
starboard		stationery	
starch		statist	
stare		statistical	
stark		statistician	
starlight		statistics	
starling		statuary	
starry		statue	
start		statuesque	
starter		stature	
startle		status	
startling		statute	
starvation		statutory	
starve		staunch	
state		stave	
State		stay	
stateliness		stead	
stately		steadfast	
statement		steadfastness	
stateroom		steadily	
statesman		steady	
statesmanlike		steak	
statesmanship		steal	
static		stealth	
statical		stealthy	
statics		steam	

steamboat		sterile	
steamer		sterility	
steamship		sterling	
steed		stern	
steel		sternum	
steelyard		stertorous	
steep		stertorousness	
steeple		stethoscope	
steepness		stethoscopic	
steer		stevedore	
steerage		stew	
steersman		steward	
stellar		stewardess	
stellate		stewardship	
stem		stick	
stench		stickler	
stencil		stiff	
stencilling		stiffen	
stenographer		stiffness	
stenography		stifle	
stenotype		stigma	
stentorian		stigmatize	
step		stile	
stepmother		stiletto	
steppe		still	
stepping		stillness	
stereoscope		stillroom	
stereotype		stilt	

Word	Outline	Word	Outline
stimulant		stolen	
stimulate		stolid	
stimulation		stolidity	
stimulative		stolidness	
stimuli		stomach	
stimulus		stomacher	
sting		stone	
stingy		stony	
stink		stood	
stint		stool	
stipend		stoop	
stipendiary		stop	
stipulate		stopgap	
stipulation		stoppage	
stir		stopper	
stirrup		stopping	
stitch		storage	
stoat		store	
stock		storehouse	
stockade		storekeeper	
stocking		stork	
stockings		storm	
stoic		stormy	
stoical		story	
stoke		stout	
stokehole		stove	
stoker		stow	
stole		stowage	

stowaway	*so—a*	stratify	*slf*
straddle	*sdl*	stratum	*sl—*
straggle	*sgl*	stratus	*slx*
straggler	*sglr*	straw	*sa*
straight	*sa*	strawberry	*saby*
straighten	*san*	stray	*sa*
straighter	*sar*	streak	*sek*
straightforward	*saf/*	stream	*se*
straightness	*sa'*	streamer	*ser*
straightway	*sa—a*	street	*sl*
strain	*sn*	strength	*s*
strainer	*snr*	strengthen	*sn*
strait	*sa*	strenuous	*snx*
strand	*s——*	stress	*s'*
strange	*sy*	stretch	*sc*
strangely	*syl*	stretcher	*scr*
strangeness	*sy'*	strew	*su*
stranger	*syr*	strewn	*sn*
strangle	*sgl*	stricken	*skn*
strangulation	*sgl*	strict	*sk*
strap	*sp*	strictness	*sk'*
strata	*sla*	stricture	*sku*
stratagem	*sly—*	stride	*sd*
strategic	*slyk*	strident	*sd-*
strategical	*slyK*	stridently	*sd-l*
strategist	*sly,*	strife	*sf*
strategy	*sly,*	strike	*sk*
stratification	*slf*	striker	*skr*

257

string	*(shorthand)*	stubbornness	*(shorthand)*
stringency	*(shorthand)*	stucco	*(shorthand)*
stringent	*(shorthand)*	stuck	*(shorthand)*
stringy	*(shorthand)*	stud	*(shorthand)*
strip	*(shorthand)*	student	*(shorthand)*
stripe	*(shorthand)*	studied	*(shorthand)*
stripling	*(shorthand)*	studio	*(shorthand)*
strive	*(shorthand)*	studious	*(shorthand)*
striving	*(shorthand)*	study	*(shorthand)*
strode	*(shorthand)*	stuff	*(shorthand)*
stroke	*(shorthand)*	stultify	*(shorthand)*
stroll	*(shorthand)*	stumble	*(shorthand)*
strong	*(shorthand)*	stumbling-block	*(shorthand)*
stronger	*(shorthand)*	stump	*(shorthand)*
stronghold	*(shorthand)*	stun	*(shorthand)*
strove	*(shorthand)*	stung	*(shorthand)*
struck	*(shorthand)*	stunk	*(shorthand)*
structural	*(shorthand)*	stunt	*(shorthand)*
structurally	*(shorthand)*	stuntedness	*(shorthand)*
structure	*(shorthand)*	stupefaction	*(shorthand)*
struggle	*(shorthand)*	stupefy	*(shorthand)*
strum	*(shorthand)*	stupendous	*(shorthand)*
strung	*(shorthand)*	stupendousness	*(shorthand)*
strut	*(shorthand)*	stupid	*(shorthand)*
strychnine	*(shorthand)*	stupidity	*(shorthand)*
stub	*(shorthand)*	stupor	*(shorthand)*
stubble	*(shorthand)*	sturdiness	*(shorthand)*
stubborn	*(shorthand)*	sturdy	*(shorthand)*

Word	Outline	Word	Outline
sturgeon		submerge	
stutter		submergence	
sty		submersion	
style		submission	
stylish		submissive	
stylist		submit	
stylus		submitted	
styptic		subordinate	
suave		subordination	
suavity		suborn	
subaltern		subornation	
subaqueous		subpoena	
subdivide		subscribe	
subdivision		subscriber	
subdue		subscription	
subject		subsequence	
subjection		subsequent	
subjective		subsequently	
subjoin		subservience	
subjugate		subservient	
subjugation		subside	
subjunctive		subsidence	
sublease		subsidiary	
sublimate		subsidize	
sublime		subsidy	
sublimity		subsist	
sublunary		subsistence	
submarine		subsoil	

substance		successful	
substantial		succession	
substantiality		successive	
substantially		successor	
substantiate		succinct	
substantive		succour	
substitute		succulent	
substitution		succumb	
substitutional		such	
substitutionary		suck	
substrata		suckle	
substructure		suckling	
subtenant		suction	
subterfuge		sudden	
subterranean		suddenly	
subtle		suddenness	
subtlety		suds	
subtract		sue	
subtraction		suede	
suburb		suet	
suburban		suffer	
subvention		sufferable	
subversion		sufferance	
subversive		sufferer	
subvert		suffering	
subway		suffice	
succeed		sufficiency	
success		sufficient	

Word	Outline	Word	Outline
sufficiently		sulphur	
suffix		sulphuretted	
suffocate		sulphuric	
suffocation		sulphurous	
suffragan		sultan	
suffrage		sultana	
suffragette		sultriness	
suffuse		sultry	
suffusion		sum	
sugar		summarily	
sugary		summarize	
suggest		summary	
suggestion		summation	
suggestive		summer	
suicidal		summit	
suicide		summon	
suit		sumptuous	
suitability		sun	
suitable		sunbeam	
suite		sunburn	
suitor		Sunday	
sulk		sunder	
sulkiness		sundown	
sulky		sundry	
sullen		sunflower	
sullenness		sung	
sully		sunk	
sulphate		sunken	

sunless		superiority	
sunlight		superlative	
sunny		superman	
sunrise		supernatural	
sunset		supernumerary	
sunshine		superposition	
sup		superscription	
superabound		supersede	
superabundance		supersonic	
superabundant		superstition	
superannuate		superstitious	
superannuation		superstructure	
superb		supervene	
superciliary		supervise	
supercilious		supervision	
superficial		supervisor	
superficiality		supine	
superfine		supper	
superfluity		supplant	
superfluous		supple	
superhuman		supplement	
superimpose		supplementary	
superimposed		suppliant	
superincumbent		supplicate	
superintend		supplication	
superintendence		supplicatory	
superintendent		supply	
superior		support	

262

supportable		surmount	
supporter		surmountable	
suppose		surname	
supposed		surpass	
supposition		surpassable	
suppress		surplice	
suppressible		surplus	
suppression		surprise	
suppressive		surrender	
suppressor		surreptitious	
suppurate		surrogate	
supremacy		surround	
supreme		surtax	
surcharge		surveillance	
sure		survey	
surely		surveyor	
sureness		survival	
surety		survive	
surf		survivor	
surface		susceptibility	
surfeit		susceptible	
surge		susceptive	
surgeon		suspect	
surgery		suspend	
surgical		suspender	
surliness		suspense	
surly		suspension	
surmise		suspensory	

Word	Shorthand	Word	Shorthand
suspicion		sweetheart	
suspicious		sweetness	
sustain		swell	
sustenance		swelter	
suture		swept	
swab		swerve	
swag		swift	
swallow		swiftness	
swam		swill	
swamp		swim	
swan		swimmer	
swap		swimming	
swarm		swimmingly	
swarthy		swindle	
swastika		swindler	
swathe		swindling	
sway		swine	
swear		swing	
sweat		swinish	
sweater		swirl	
sweep		switch	
sweeper		switchboard	
sweeping		swivel	
sweepstake		swollen	
sweet		swoon	
sweetbread		swoop	
sweeten		sword	
sweeter		swordsman	

swordsmanship	s//~ß	symposium	~pz~
swore	s-o	symptom	~~~
sworn	s-rn	symptomatic	s~J
swum	s~	symptomatical	s~lK
swung	s-q	synagogue	sngq
sycamore	sk~o	synchronize	sqr3
sycophancy	skf	syncopate	sqpa
sycophant	skf-	syncope	sqp,
sycophantic	sf-k	syndicate	s—ka
syllabic	sllbk	synod	snd
syllable	sllb	synonym	snn~
syllogism	slz~	synonymous	snn~x
syllogistic	slzS	synopsis	snpss
sylph	slf	syntactic	s-kJ
sylvan	slvn	syntax	s-x
symbol	s~b	synthesis	snlss
symbolic	s~bll	synthetic	snlJ
symbolical	s~blK	syphon	sfn
symbolism	s~bz~	syringe	sry
symbolize	s~bz	syrup	srp
symmetrical	sNeK	systaltic	sslJ
symmetry	sNe,	system	ss~
sympathetic	s~plJ	systematic	ss~J
sympathize	s~plz	systematical	ss~lK
sympathy	s~pl,	systematically	ss~lK
symphonic	s~fnk	systematize	ss~lz
symphony	s~fn,	systole	ssle

265

tab	Ub	tadpole	Ldpl
tabard	Ub/	taffeta	Ufla
tabby	Ub,	tag	Lq
tabernacle	IbnK	tail	Lol
table	Lab	tailor	Il
tableaux	Ubo	tailoress	Il'
tablecloth	Ubkll	taint	La-
tablespoon	Ubsn	take	Lk
tablespoonful	Ubsnf	taking	Lk
tablet	Ubl	talcum	Llk
tableware	Ub-a	tale	Lol
taboo	Ubu	talent	Ul-
tabular	Ibl	talisman	Ulz-
tabulate	Ubla	talk	Lak
tabulation	Ubl	talkative	Lkv
tabulator	Ibla	talker	Ik
tacit	Lsl	tall	Lol
taciturn	Lsln	taller	Il
taciturnity	Lsln)	tallness	Ul'
tack	Lk	tallow	Llo
tackle	LK	tally	Ul,
tact	Lk	talon	Uln
tactical	LlK	tameable	Lab
tactician	Lkj	tamarind	I--
tactics	LlV	tamarisk	Insk
tactile	Lkl	tambourine	Iubn

266

tame		tarantula	
tameness		tardiness	
tamper		tardy	
tan		tare	
tandem		target	
tang		tariff	
tangent		tarn	
tangential		tarnish	
tangibility		tarpaulin	
tangible		tarry	
tangle		tart	
tank		tartan	
tankard		tartar	
tanner		tartaric	
tannery		task	
tannic		taskmaster	
tannin		tassel	
tantalize		taste	
tantamount		tastefully	
tap		tasteless	
tape		taster	
taper		tasty	
tapestry		tatter	
tapeworm		tattle	
tapioca		tattoo	
tapping		taught	
tapster		taunt	
tar		tautological	

Word	Shorthand	Word	Shorthand
tautology		technologist	
tavern		technology	
tawdriness		tedious	
tawdry		tedium	
tawny		tee	
tax		teem	
taxation		teenager	
taxicab		teeth	
taximeter		teetotal	
tea		teetotaler	
teach		telegram	
teachable		telegrapher	
teacher		telegraphic	
teak		telegraphist	
team		telegraphy	
teamster		telepathy	
teapot		telephone	
tear (v)		telephonic	
tear		telescope	
tearful		telescopic	
tearless		television	
tease		tell	
teaspoon		teller	
teat		temerity	
technical		temper	
technicality		temperament	
technique		temperance	
technological		temperate	

268

temperature		tenet	
tempest		tenfold	
tempestuous		tennis	
temple		tenon	
temporal		tenor	
temporality		tenpence	
temporary		tense	
temporize		tensile	
tempt		tension	
temptation		tent	
tempter		tentacle	
tempting		tentative	
ten		tenth	
tenable		tenuous	
tenacious		tenure	
tenacity		tepid	
tenancy		tepidness	
tenant		tercentenary	
tenantry		teredo	
tench		term	
tend		termagant	
tendency		terminable	
tender		terminal	
tenderness		terminate	
tendon		termination	
tendril		terminology	
tenebrous		terminus	
tenement		tern	

269

D.—S

terrace		tetanus	
terracotta		tether	
terrain		tetragon	
terrestrial		tetrahedron	
terrible		tetralogy	
terrier		text	
terrific		textile	
terrify		texture	
territorial		than	
territory		thank	
terror		thankful	
terse		thankfulness	
tersely		thankless	
terseness		thanksgiving	
tertian		that	
tertiary		thatch	
tesselation		thaw	
test		the	
testament		theatre	
testamentary		theatrical	
testate		theft	
testator		their	
testatrix		theism	
tester		theist	
testify		theistic	
testimonial		them	
testimony		theme	
testy		themselves	

then	⌐n	thesaurus	⌐src
thence	✓	these	⌐ʒ
thenceforth	✓ʄ	thesis	⌐ss
thenceforward	✓ʄ/	they	⌐y
theocracy	⌐eks,	they'll	⌐yℓ
theodolite	⌐edℓe	they're	⌐yᵣ
theologian	⌐eoℓn	they've	⌐yᵥ
theological	⌐eoℓK	thick	⌐k
theology	⌐eoℓ	thicken	⌐kn
theorem	⌐e⌐	thicker	⌐k
theoretic	⌐eⱼ	thicket	⌐kℓ
theoretical	⌐eℓK	thickness	⌐k'
theorist	⌐e,	thief	⌐f
theorize	⌐eʒ	thieve	⌐e
theory	⌐ey	thievish	⌐eʒ
theosophist	⌐esf,	thigh	⌐
theosophy	⌐esf,	thimble	⌐b
therapeutic	⌐pⱼ	thin	⌐n
there	⌐	thing	⌐q
thereabout	⌐ab	think	⌐q
thereafter	⌐af	thinker	⌐q
thereby	⌐b	thinner	⌐n
therefore	⌐ƒ	thinness	⌐n'
thermal	⌐ℓ	third	ʒd
thermodynamics	⌐dⱼks	thirst	⌐,
thermometer	⌐e	thirsty	⌐s,
thermometric	⌐ek	thirteen	13
thermometrical	⌐eK	thirteenth	13L

271

thirtieth	30ι	three	ϳ
thirty	30	threefold	ϳfol
this	Uh	threepence	3ρ
thistle	bsl	threeply	ϳ —pι
thither	Iι	threescore	ϳ ιsko
thong	lq	thresh	U3
thorax	bιx	threshold	U3hl
thorn	bιn	threw	Zu
thorough	bιo	thrift	Ψ
thoroughbred	bιobd	thriftless	Ψlι'
thoroughfare	bιofa	thrifty	Ψ,
thoroughgoing	bιoq	thrill	Zι
thoroughness	bιo'	thrive	Zι.
those	los	throat	Zo
though	lo	throb	Zb
thought	tt	throe	Zo
thoughtful	ttf	throne	Zn
thoughtless	ttι'	throng	Zq
thousand	J	throttle	Ztι
thousandfold	Jfol	through	Zu
thousandth	Iι	throughout	Zu⌣
thrall	Zal	throw	Zo
thrash	U3	thrown	Zn
thread	Zd	thrush	U3
threadbare	Zdba	thrust	Z,
threat	Zt	thud	ld
threaten	Ztn	thug	lq
threatening	Ztn	thuggery	lqч

Word	Outline	Word	Outline
thumb		tightness	
thump		tigress	
thumper		tile	
thumping		till	
thunder		tiller	
thunderbolt		tilt	
thunderous		timber	
thunderstorm		timbre	
thunderstruck		time	
thundery		timeliness	
Thursday		timely	
thus		timeworn	
thwart		timid	
thyme		timidity	
tiara		timorous	
tick		tin	
ticket		tincture	
tickle		tinder	
tidal		tinfoil	
tide		tinge	
tideway		tingle	
tidings		tinker	
tidy		tinkle	
tie		tinsel	
tier		tint	
tiger		tiny	
tight		tip	
tighten		tipple	

273

Word	Outline	Word	Outline
tirade		token	
tire		told	
tiresome		tolerable	
tissue		tolerant	
tit		tolerate	
titanic		toleration	
tithe		toll	
titillate		tomahawk	
titillation		tomato	
title		tomb	
titter		tombstone	
tittle		tome	
titular		tomfoolery	
to		tomorrow	
toad		ton	
toadstool		tone	
toady		tongs	
toast		tongue	
tobacco		tonic	
tobacconist		tonight	
toboggan		tonnage	
today		tonsil	
toddle		tonsillitis	
toe		tonsure	
toga		tontine	
together		too	
toil		took	
toilet		tool	

274

Word	Shorthand	Word	Shorthand
toot	*lu*	torrid	*lrd*
tooth	*lul*	torsion	*ly*
toothache	*ttk*	tortoise	*l/s*
toothbrush	*ttbʒ*	torture	*l/u*
toothpaste	*ttp,*	tory	*ly*
toothpick	*ttpk*	toss	*l'*
top	*lp*	tot	*tt*
topaz	*lpʒ*	total	*ttl*
topic	*lpk*	totality	*ttl)*
topical	*lpK*	totally	*ttl*
topmost	*lp⌐,*	totem	*tt⌐*
topographic	*lpgfk*	totter	*Io*
topographical	*lpgfK*	touch	*lc*
topography	*lpgf,*	touchiness	*lc'*
topple	*lp*	tough	*ly*
topsy-turvy	*lpsbv,*	tour	*lu*
torch	*lrc*	tourist	*lu,*
tore	*lo*	tournament	*lrn-*
torment	*lr-*	tourniquet	*lrka*
tormentor	*Jr-*	tout	*Ll*
torn	*lrn*	tow	*lo*
tornado	*lrndo*	towage	*lor*
torpedo	*lrpdo*	towards	*l//*
torpid	*lrpd*	towel	*Ll*
torpidity	*lrpd)*	towelling	*Ll*
torpor	*Jrp*	tower	*I*
torque	*lrk*	town	*Ln*
torrent	*lr-*	township	*Lnʒ*

275

toxic		train	
toxicology		trainer	
toy		trait	
trace		traitor	
traceable		traitorous	
tracery		traitress	
trachea		trajectory	
tracheotomy		tram	
tracing		trammel	
track		tramp	
tract		trample	
tractability		trance	
tractable		tranquil	
traction		tranquillize	
tractor		tranquillity	
trade		transact	
trader		transaction	
tradesman		transalpine	
tradition		transatlantic	
traditional		transcend	
traditionary		transcendent	
traduce		transcendental	
traffic		transcribe	
tragedian		transcript	
tragedy		transcription	
tragic		transept	
tragical		transfer	
trail		transferable	

transference	𝓘𝒇	transmittal	𝓘𝓁𝓁
transferring	𝓘𝒇	transmutable	𝓘𝓊𝒷
transfiguration	𝓘𝒇ℊ𝟣	transmutation	𝓘𝓊𝓎
transfigure	𝓘𝒇ℊ	transmute	𝓘𝓊
transfigurement	𝓘𝒇ℊ-	transparence	𝓘𝓅✓
transfix	𝓘𝒇𝓍	transparency	𝓘𝓅✓
transform	𝓘𝒇	transparent	𝓘𝓅- 逐水流，以法法 坦白法
transformation	𝓘𝒇𝓎	transpire	𝓘𝓅𝓊
transformer	𝒥𝓎	transplant	𝓘𝓅-
transfuse	𝓘𝒇𝟥	transport	𝓘𝓅 /
transfusion	𝓘𝒇𝟣	transportation	𝓘𝓅/𝟣
transgress	𝓘ℊ'	transposal	𝓘𝓅𝔃𝓁
transgression	𝓘ℊ𝟣	transpose	𝓘𝓅𝟥
transgressor	𝓘ℊ'	transposition	𝓘𝓅𝔃𝟣
transient	𝒥-	transubstantiation	𝓘𝓈𝓈𝟣
transit	𝓘𝓁	transverse	𝓘𝓋𝓇𝓈
transition	𝓎	trap	𝓎𝓅
transitive	𝓘𝓋	trapeze	𝓎𝓅𝟥
transitory	𝓘𝓁𝓎	trapping	𝓎𝓅
translate	𝓘𝓁𝓪	trash	𝓋𝟥
translation	𝓘𝓁𝓎	trashy	𝓋𝟥,
translucency	𝓘𝓁𝓈✓	travail	𝓊𝓁
translucent	𝓘𝓁𝓈-	travel	𝓊𝓁
transmigrate	𝓘ℊ𝓪	traveller	𝓎𝓋𝓁
transmigration	𝓘ℊ𝟣	traverse	𝓋𝓇𝓈
transmissible	𝓘𝓈𝒷	travesty	𝓋𝓈,
transmission	𝓘𝓎	trawl	𝓁𝓪𝓁
transmit	𝓘𝓁	trawler	𝓎𝓁

277

tray		trepan	
treacherous		trepidation	
treachery		trespass	
treacle		tresses	
tread		trestle	
treadle		triad	
treadmill		trial	
treason		triangle	
treasonable		triangular	
treasure		triangulate	
treasurer		triangulation	
treasury		tribal	
treat		tribe	
treatise		tribulation	
treatment		tribunal	
treaty		tribune	
treble		tributary	
tree		tribute	
trefoil		trice	
trellis		tricentenary	
tremble		trichinosis	
tremendous		trick	
tremor		trickery	
tremulous		trickle	
trench		trickster	
trenchant		tricky	
trencher		tricolour	
trend		tricycle	

278

trident		tripos	
tried		trisect	
triennial		trisection	
tries		trisyllabic	
trifle		trisyllable	
trifling		trite	
trifoliate		triturable	
trig		triturate	
trigger		trituration	
triglyph		triumph	
trigonometric		triumphal	
trigonometrical		triumphant	
trigonometry		triumvir	
trilingual		triumvirate	
trill		triune	
trillion		trivial	
trilogy		triviality	
trim		trochee	
trinity		trod	
trinket		trodden	
trio		troglodyte	
trip		troll	
tripartite		trolley	
tripe		trombone	
triple		troop	
triplet		troops	
triplicate		trope	
tripod		trophy	

tropic	𝓛pk	truncate	𝓛ga
tropical	𝓛pK	truncheon	𝓛cn
trot	tt	trundle	𝓛—l
troubadour	𝓛bdo	trunk	𝓛q
trouble	𝓛b	truss	𝓛'
troublesome	𝓛bs	trust	𝓛,
trough	𝓛	trustee	𝓛se
trounce	𝓛	trustful	𝓛sf
trousers	𝓛zs	trustworthiness	𝓛srl'
trousseau	𝓛so	trustworthy	𝓛srl,
trout	𝓛t	trusty	𝓛s,
trowel	𝓛l	truth	𝓛ul
troy	𝓛y	truthful	ttf
truant	𝓛u-	truthfulness	ttf'
truce	𝓛us	truthless	ttl'
truck	𝓛k	try	𝓛
truckle	𝓛K	tsetse	tts,
truculence	𝓛kl	tub	lb
truculent	𝓛kl-	tube	lub
trudge	𝓛	tuber	lb
true	𝓛u	tubercle	lbkl
truer	𝓛u	tuberculosis	lbklss
truffle	𝓛fl	tuberculous	lbklx
truism	𝓛uz	tubular	lbl
truly	𝓛ul	tuck	lk
trumpery	𝓛py	Tuesday	lu
trumpet	𝓛pl	tuft	𝓛
trumpeter	𝓛pl	tufty	𝓛,

280

tug		turfy	
tuition		turgid	
tulip		turkey	
tulle		turmoil	
tumble		turn	
tumbler		turnery	
tumbrel		turning	
tumid		turnip	
tumour		turnover	
tumult		turnpike	
tumultuary		turnstile	
tumultuous		turpentine	
tumulus		turpitude	
tun		turquoise	
tune		turret	
tuneful		turtle	
tuneless		tusk	
tunic		tussle	
tunnel		tutelage	
tunny		tutor	
turban		tutoress	
turbid		tutorial	
turbine		tutorship	
turbot		tweak	
turbulence		tweed	
turbulent		tweezers	
tureen		twelfth	
turf		twelve	

twelvemonth	12 〜o	type	
twentieth	20 ∟	typewriter	
twenty	20	typewriting	
twice		typhoid	
twig		typhoon	
twilight		typhus	
twill		typical	
twin		typify	
twine		typist	
twinge		typographic	
twinkle		typographical	
twirl		typography	
twist		tyrannic	
twit		tyrannical	
twitch		tyrannize	
twitter		tyrannous	
two	2	tyranny	
twofold	2 fol	tyrant	
tycoon		tyro	

U

ubiquitous		ulcerate	
ubiquity		ulceration	
udder		ulcerous	
ugliness		ulster	
ugly		ulterior	
ukulele		ultimate	
ulcer		ultimatum	

ultimo		unalloyed	
ultramarine		unalterable	
ultramontane		unambitious	
umber		unamiable	
umbilical		unanimity	
umbilicus		unanimous	
umbrage		unanswerable	
umbrella		unappalled	
umpire		unappreciated	
unabashed		unapproachable	
unabated		unapt	
unable		unarm	
unabridged		unasked	
unaccented		unassailable	
unacceptable		unassuming	
unaccommodating		unattached	
unaccompanied		unattainable	
unaccountable		unattended	
unaccustomed		unattractive	
unacknowledged		unauthorized	
unacquainted		unavailable	
unadorned		unavailing	
unadulterated		unavoidable	
unadvisable		unaware	
unadvised		unbalanced	
unaffected		unbar	
unafraid		unbearable	
unaided		unbecoming	

unbegotten	ubgln	unchanged	ucj
unbelief	ublf	uncharitable	ucrlb
unbend	ub —	unchaste	uc,
unbending	ub —=	unchecked	uck
unbiased	ubn,	unchurch	ucrc
unbidden	ubdn	uncial	ux
unbind	ubn —	unciform	usf
unbelieving	uble	uncircumcised	uCsz
unbleached	ubē	uncircumspect	uCsk
unblemished	ub~zʒ	uncivil	usvl
unblessed	ub,	uncivilized	usvlz
unblushing	ubʒ	unclasp	ukls
unbolt	ubll	uncle	uql
unborn	ubrn	unclean	ukln
unbound	ub⌣ —	unclosed	uklz
unbounded	ub⌣ —=	unclothed	uklī
unbrace	ubs	unclouded	ukl_d
unbreakable	ubkb	uncoil	ukyl
unbridled	ubdl	uncomely	ukl
unbroken	ubkn	uncomfortable	ukf//b
unbuckle	ubK	uncommon	ukn
unburden	ub/n	uncomplaining	ukpn
unbutton	ubln	uncompromising	ukp~z
uncalled	uklī	unconcerned	uksn̄
unceasing	uss̱	unconditional	ukdjl
uncertain	us/n	uncongenial	ukjnl
uncertainty	us/-,	unconnected	uknk
unchain	ucn	unconquerable	uKqb

284

Word	Shorthand	Word	Shorthand
unconscionable		underbid	
unconscious		undercurrent	
unconsidered		undercut	
unconstitutional		underdone	
unconstrained		underestimate	
uncontested		underfoot	
uncontrollable		undergo	
unconverted		underground	
uncork		undergrowth	
uncounted		underhand	
uncouple		underlay	
uncouth		underline	
uncover		underling	
uncrowned		undermine	
unction		undermost	
unctuous		underneath	
uncultivated		underpaid	
uncurl		underpin	
uncut		underrate	
undaunted		underscore	
undeceive		undersell	
undecided		undershirt	
undefended		undersigned	
undefiled		undersized	
undefined		understand	
undelivered		understanding	
undeniable		understood	
under		understudy	

285

D.—T

undertake	undone
undertaker	undoubted
undertaking	undress
undertone	undulate
undertook	undulation
undervalue	undulatory
underwear	unduly
underwent	undutiful
underwrite	undying
undeserved	unearned
undesigned	unearth
undesirable	unearthly
undetected	uneasy
undetermined	uneducated
undeviating	unembarrassed
undigested	unembodied
undignified	unemployed
undiminished	unending
undiscernible	unengaged
undiscerning	unenlightened
undisciplined	unenviable
undisguised	unenvied
undismayed	unequal
undisputed	unequivocal
undisturbed	unerring
undivided	unessential
undo	uneven
undoing	uneventful

unexampled		unforeseen	
unexceptionable		unforetold	
unexhausted		unforgiving	
unexpected		unformed	
unexplained		unfortunate	
unexplored		unfounded	
unexpressed		unfrequented	
unfaded		unfriendly	
unfailing		unfruitful	
unfair		unfulfilled	
unfaithfulness		unfurl	
unfamiliar		unfurnished	
unfashionable		ungainly	
unfasten		ungentle	
unfathomable		ungird	
unfavourable		ungodly	
unfeeling		ungracious	
unfeigned		ungrateful	
unfelt		ungrounded	
unfettered		ungruding	
unfilial		unguarded	
unfinished		unguent	
unfit		unhallowed	
unflagging		unhand	
unflattering		unhandy	
unfledged		unhappy	
unflinching		unharmed	
unfold		unharnessed	

287

unhealthy		unite	
unheard		unity	
unheeding		universal	
unhesitating		universality	
unhinge		universe	
unholy		university	
unhonoured		unjust	
unhook		unkempt	
unhorse		unkept	
unhurt		unkind	
unicorn		unkindness	
unification		unknown	
uniform		unlawful	
uniformity		unlearn	
uniformly		unlearned	
unify		unless	
unilateral		unlettered	
unimpaired		unlike	
unimpeachable		unload	
unimportant		unlock	
unimproved		unlocked	
uninjured		unloose	
unintelligible		unloving	
uninterrupted		unlucky	
union		unmake	
unique		unmeaning	
unison		unmoor	
unit		unmount	

288

Word	Shorthand	Word	Shorthand
unmounted		unreasonable	
unmoved		unrest	
unmuffle		unrestrained	
unmuzzle		unrighteous	
unnatural		unrighteousness	
unnecessary		unruly	
unnerve		unsafe	
unnoticed		unsaid	
unoccupied		unsay	
unopened		unscathed	
unpack		unscrew	
unpaid		unscrupulous	
unparalleled		unsearchable	
unpeople		unseat	
unpitied		unseemly	
unpleasant		unseen	
unprecedented		unselfish	
unpretending		unsettled	
unprincipled		unshaken	
unprofitable		unsheathe	
unpunished		unship	
unqualified		unsightly	
unquestionable		unskilful	
unquestioned		unsought	
unquiet		unsound	
unravel		unspeakable	
unreal		unspotted	
unreason		unstable	

unstained	*usn̄*	unwearable	*uᴗab*
unsteady	*usd,*	unwearying	*uᴗy*
unstop	*usp*	unweave	*uᴗe*
unsuccessful	*usuc*	unwed	*uᴗd*
unsuitable	*usub*	unwelcome	*uᴗlk*
unsuspected	*ussk*	unwept	*uᴗp*
untaught	*utt*	unwieldy	*uᴗld,*
unteachable	*ulcb*	unwilling	*ul̠*
unthinking	*ulq*	unwind	*uᴗ—*
unthread	*uld*	unwise	*uᴗ3*
untidy	*uld,*	unwittingly	*uᴗtl*
untie	*uli*	unworthy	*uᴗrl,*
until	*ul*	unwoven	*uᴗon*
untimely	*ulil*	unwrap	*urp*
untiring	*uli̠*	unyoke	*uyk*
untold	*ulol*	up	*p*
untouched	*ulē*	upbraid	*pbd*
untoward	*ul/*	upbraiding	*pbd̠*
untried	*ulī*	upheaval	*phel*
untrodden	*uldn*	upheave	*phe*
untrue	*ulu*	upheld	*phl*
untruth	*utt*	uphill	*phl*
unturned	*uln̄*	uphold	*phol*
untwine	*ulᴖn*	upholster	*phls*
unusual	*ux*	upholstery	*phls,*
unveil	*uvl*	upland	*pl —*
unwarped	*uᴗp̄*	uplift	*plf*
unwary	*uᴗy*	upon	*pn*

upper	P	usage	usy
uppermost	P~,	use	us u3
upright	pru	useful	usf
uprightness	pru'	useless	usl'
uprise	prz	usher	U3
uprising	prz	using	u3
uproar	pro	usual	x
uproarious	prox	usurer	Uzu
uproot	pru	usurp	usp
upset	psl	usurpation	uspy
upshoot	pzu	usurious	uzyx
upside-down	psd n	usury	uzy
upstairs	psas	utensil	ul/l
upstart	pSl	utilitarian	ullyn
upward	p/	utilitarianism	ullynz
urban	ubn	utility	ull)
urbane	ubn	utilize	ullz
urbanity	ubn)	utmost	ul~,
urchin	ucn	utopia	ulpa
urge	uy	utter	U
urgency	uy/	utterable	Ub
urgent	uy-	utterance	U/
urn	un	utterly	Ul
us	us	uttermost	Un,
U.S.	US	uvula	uvla
usable	uzb	uxorious	uxyx

vacancy		valedictory	
vacant		valentine	
vacate		valerian	
vacation		valet	
vaccinate		valetudinarian	
vaccination		valiant	
vaccine		valiantly	
vacillate		valid	
vacillation		validity	
vacillatory		valise	
vacuity		valley	
vacuous		valorous	
vacuum		valour	
vagabond		valuable	
vagabondage		valuation	
vagabondism		valuator	
vagary		value	
vagrancy		valued	
vagrant		valve	
vague		valvular	
vagueness		vamp	
vain		vampire	
vainglorious		van	
valance		vandalism	
vale		vane	
valediction		vanguard	

292

vanilla	*vnla*	vaticinate	*vlsna*
vanish	*vnʒ*	vaticination	*vlsny*
vanity	*vn)*	vaudeville	*vdvl*
vanquish	*vqʒ*	vault	*vll*
vantage	*v−ı*	vaunt	*va−*
vapid	*vpd*	veal	*vel*
vapidity	*vpd)*	veer	*ve*
vaporization	*vpʒı*	vegetable	*vɉlb*
vaporize	*vpʒ*	vegetarian	*vɉlyn*
vaporous	*vpx*	vegetarianism	*vɉlynɉ*
vapory	*vpч*	vegetate	*vɉla*
vapour	*Vp*	vegetation	*vɉч*
variable	*vyb*	vegetative	*vɉlv*
variance	*vy*	vehemence	*⌣*
variant	*vч−*	vehement	*ve−*
variation	*vyч*	vehicle	*vK*
varicose	*vrks*	vehicular	*Vkl*
variegated	*vygā*	veil	*val*
variety	*vr)*	vein	*vn*
various	*vyx*	vellum	*vl⌣*
varnish	*vrnʒ*	velocity	*vls)*
vary	*vч*	velvet	*vlvl*
vase	*vʒ*	velveteen	*vlvln*
vassal	*vsl*	velvety	*vlvl,*
vast	*v,*	venal	*vnl*
vastness	*vs'*	venality	*vnl)*
vat	*vl*	vend	*v——*
Vatican	*vlkn*	vendetta	*v——la*

293

vendible		veracity	
vendor		verandah	
veneer		verb	
veneering		verbal	
venerable		verbatim	
venerate		verbena	
veneration		verbiage	
Venetian		verbose	
vengeance		verbosity	
vengeful		verdant	
venial		verdict	
venison		verdigris	
venom		verdure	
venomous		verge	
vent		verger	
ventilate		verifiable	
ventilation		verification	
ventilator		verify	
ventral		verisimilitude	
ventricle		veritable	
ventriloquism		verity	
ventriloquist		vermicelli	
ventriloquy		vermicide	
venture		vermiform	
venturesome		vermilion	
venturous		vermin	
venue		vernacular	
veracious		vernal	

294

vernier		veteran	
versatile		veterinary	
versatility		veto	
verse		vex	
versification		vexation	
versify		vexatious	
version		via	
versus		viable	
vertebra		viaduct	
vertebrae		vial	
vertebral		viaticum	
vertebrate		vibrate	
vertex		vibration	
vertical		vibratory	
vertigo		vicar	
verve		vicarage	
very		vicarial	
vesicle		vicarious	
vesicular		vice	
vesper		vicegerent	
vessel		viceregal	
vest		viceroy	
vestal		vicinity	
vestibule		vicious	
vestige		vicissitude	
vestment		victim	
vestry		victimize	
vesture		victor	

victorious	vkyx	vintage	v—y
victory	vky	viola	vla
victual	vll	violable	vlb
view	vu	violate	vla
viewless	vul'	violation	vly
vigil	vzl	violator	Vla
vigilance	vzl/	violence	vl/
vigilant	vzl-	violent	vl-
vignette	vnl	violet	vll
vigorous	Vgx	violin	vln
vigour	Vq	violinist	vln,
vile	vrl	violoncello	vlclo
vileness	vl'	viper	Vp
vilify	vlf	viperous	vpx
villa	vla	virago	vrq
village	vly	virgin	vyn
villager	Vly	virginal	vynl
villain	vln	virginity	vyn)
villainous	vlnx	viridity	vrd)
villainy	vln,	virile	vrl
vindicate	v——ka	virility	vrl)
vindication	v——ky	virtual	v/ul
vindicator	V——ko	virtually	v/ul
vindictive	v——kv	virtue	v/u
vine	vrn	virtuoso	v/uso
vinegar	Vnq	virtuous	v/ux
vinery	vrny	virulence	vrl/
vineyard	vny/	virulent	vrl-

virus	᠕ᡄᡆ	vituperative	᠕ᠯᠠᡤ
visage	᠕ᡔᠯ	vivacious	᠕᠕ᡆ
viscera	᠕ᡔᠠ	vivacity	᠕᠕᠊)
viscid	᠕ᡔᡑ	vivid	᠕᠕ᡑ
viscidity	᠕ᡔᡑ)	vividness	᠕᠕ᡑ'
viscosity	᠕ᡔᡐᡔ)	vivify	᠕᠕ᡶ
viscount	᠕ᡐᡌ	viviparous	᠕᠕ᡜᡆ
viscous	᠕ᡔᡐᡆ	vivisection	᠕᠕ᡔᡐᡃ
visibility	᠕ᡔᡓᡠ)	vixen	᠕ᡆᡐ
visible	᠕ᡔᡓᡠ	vocabulary	᠕ᡌᡠᡠᡃ
vision	᠕᠊ᠯ	vocal	᠕ᡌᡠ
visionary	᠕ᡔᡃᠯ	vocalist	᠕ᡌᡠ,
visit	᠕ᡔᡓ	vocalize	᠕ᡌᡠᡔ
visitation	᠕ᡔᡃᠯ	vocation	᠕ᡜᡃ
visitor	᠕ᡔᡓ	vocative	᠕ᡌᡁ
visor	᠕᠊ᡔ	vociferous	᠕ᡔᡶᡆ
vista	᠕ᡔᠠ	vogue	᠕ᡆᡊ
visual	᠕ᡔᡠ	voice	᠕᠊ᠯ
vital	᠕ᡠ	voiceless	᠕ᡃᡠ'
vitality	᠕ᡠ)	void	᠕ᡃᡑ
vitalize	᠕ᡠᡔ	voidable	᠕ᡃᡑᡠ
vitamins	᠕ᡓᡐᡔ	voil	᠕ᡃᡠ
vitiate	᠕ᡔᠠ	volatile	᠕ᡠᡠ
vitreous	᠕ᡓᡆ	volatility	᠕ᡠᡠ)
vitrify	᠕ᡶ	volatilize	᠕ᡠᡠᡔ
vitriol	᠕ᡠ	volcanic	᠕ᡠᡌᡌ
vituperate	᠕ᡠᡜᠠ	volcano	᠕ᡠᡌᡐ
vituperation	᠕ᡠᡜᡃ	vole	᠕ᡆᡠ

volition		vortex	
volley		vortices	
volt		vote	
voltage		voter	
voluble		vouch	
volubility		voucher	
volume		vow	
voluminous		vowel	
voluntary		voyage	
voluntaryism		vulcanize	
volunteer		vulgar	
voluptuary		vulgarism	
voluptuous		vulgarity	
volute		vulgarize	
vomit		vulnerability	
voracious		vulnerable	
voracity		vulture	

W

wad		wager	
waddle		waggoner	
wade		wagon	
wafer		waif	
wafery		wail	
waffle		wailing	
waft		wainscot	
wag		waist	
wage		waistband	

298

Word	Shorthand	Word	Shorthand
waistcoat		wantonness	
wait		war	
waiter		warble	
waitress		warbler	
waive		ward	
wake		warden	
wakeful		warder	
wakefulness		wardrobe	
waken		ware	
Wales		warehouse	
walk		warfare	
walker		wariness	
wall		warlike	
wallet		warlock	
wallop		warm	
wallow		warmer	
walnut		warmth	
walrus		warn	
waltz		warning	
wan		warp	
wand		warrant	
wander		warrantable	
wanderer		warranty	
wane		warren	
want		warrior	
wanted		warship	
wanting		wart	
wanton		wary	

Word	Shorthand	Word	Shorthand
was		wave	
wash		waver	
washable		wax	
washboard		waxen	
washer		waxy	
wasn't		way	
wasp		wayfarer	
waspish		waylay	
waste		wayside	
wasteful		wayward	
waster		we	
wastrel		weak	
watch		weaken	
watcher		weaker	
watchful		weakling	
watchman		weakness	
watchword		weal	
water		weald	
watercress		wealth	
waterfall		wealthy	
waterfowl		wean	
watermelon		weapon	
waterproof		wear	
waterspout		wearable	
watery		wearer	
watt		weariness	
wattle		wearisome	
waul		weary	

300

Word	Shorthand	Word	Shorthand
weasel		welfare	
weather		well	
weatherbeaten		well (prefix)	
weathercock		we'll	
weave		well-known	
weaver		Welsh	
web		welt	
wed		welter	
wedding		wen	
wedge		wench	
wedlock		wend	
Wednesday		went	
wee		wept	
weed		were	
weedy		west	
week		westerly	
weekday		western	
weekly		westward	
weep		wet	
weevil		wetness	
weft		wettish	
weigh		we've	
weight		whack	
weighty		whale	
weir		whalebone	
weird		whaler	
welcome		wharf	
weld		wharfage	

301

wharfinger		whereupon	
wharves		wherever	
what		wherewith	
whatever		wherewithal	
whatnot		whet	
whatsoever		whether	
wheat		whetstone	
wheaten		whey	
wheedle		which	
wheel		whichever	
wheelbarrow		whichsoever	
wheelwright		whiff	
wheeze		while	
whelk		whilst	
whelp		whim	
when		whimper	
whenever		whimsy	
whensoever		whimsical	
where		whine	
whereas		whinny	
whereat		whip	
whereby		whippet	
wherefore		whirl	
wherein		whirlpool	
whereof		whirlwind	
whereon		whisk	
wheresoever		whisker	
whereto		whisky	

302

Word	Shorthand	Word	Shorthand
whisper		wicket	
whist		wide	
whistle		widely	
whit		widen	
white		wider	
whiten		widow	
whiteness		widower	
whiter		widowhood	
whitewash		width	
whither		wield	
whitlow		wieldy	
whittle		wife	
who		wifely	
whoever		wig	
whole		wild	
wholesale		wilder	
wholesome		wilderness	
wholly		wildfire	
whom		wildly	
whore		wile	
whorl		wilful	
whose		will (noun)	
whosoever		will (verb)	
why		willing	
wick		willow	
wicked		wilt	
wickedness		wily	
wicker		win	

wince		wisacre	
winch		wisely	
wind (v)		wiser	
wind		wish	
windfall		wisher	
winding		wishful	
windlass		wishfulness	
windmill		wisp	
window		wistful	
windpipe		wit	
windward		witch	
windy		witchcraft	
wine		with	
wing		withal	
wink		withdraw	
winkle		withdrawal	
winner		withdrew	
winning		wither	
winnow		withers	
winsome		withheld	
winter		withhold	
wintry		within	
wipe		without	
wire		withstand	
wireless		withstood	
wis		witless	
wisdom		witness	
wise		witty	

304

Word	Outline	Word	Outline
wives		woo	
wizard		wood	
wizen		woodbine	
wobble		woodcock	
woe		woodcutter	
woebegone		wooden	
woeful		woodland	
woke		woodman	
wold		woodpecker	
wolf		woodwork	
wolfish		woody	
wolverene		woof	
wolves		wool	
woman		woollen	
womanhood		woolly	
womanish		word	
womankind		wordiness	
womanly		wore	
womb		work	
women		workable	
won		worker	
wonder		workman	
wonderful		workmanship	
wonderfully		workshop	
wonderland		world	
wonderment		worldliness	
wondrous		worldling	
wont		worldly	

English	Shorthand	English	Shorthand
worm		wreathe	
worn ✓		wreck	
worry ✓		wren	
worse		wrench	
worship ✓	崇拜 n.	wrest	
worshipper ✓	禮拜者 n.	wrestle	
worshipping		wretch	
worst ✓		wretched	
worsted ✓	毛紗 n	wretchedness	
worth		wriggle	
worthily		wright	
worthless		wring	
worthy		wringer	
would		wrinkle	
wound (v)		wrist	
wound		writ	
wove		write	
woven		writer	
wrack		writhe	
wraith		written	
wrangle		wrong	
wrap		wrongful	
wrapper		wrote	
wrapping ✓		wroth	
wrath		wrought	
wrathful		wrung	
wreak		wry	
wreath		wryly	

X

xebec	ʒbk	xylography	ʒlgf,
X-ray	xra	xylonite	ʒlnu
xylograph	ʒlgf	xylophone	ʒlfn
xylographer	ʒlgfr	xystus	ʒsx
xylographic	ʒlgfk		

Y

yacht	yl	yeasty	ys,
yak	yk	yell	yl
yam	y⌢	yellow	ylo
Yankee	yqe	yelp	ylp
yard	y/	yeoman	y⌢ -
yardstick	y/sk	yeomanry	ynr,
yarn	yrn	yes	ys
yaw	ya	yesterday	ysd
yawl	yal	yet	yl
yawn	yan	yew	yu
yean	yn	yield	yeld
yeanling	ynlq	yielding	yeld
year	y	yodel	ydl
yearling	ylq	yoke	yok
yearly	yl	yokel	ykl
yearn	yrn	yolk	yok
yearning	yrn	yonder	y—
yeast	ye,	you	u

young	*(shorthand)*	yourself	*(shorthand)*
younger	*(shorthand)*	yourselves	*(shorthand)*
youngster	*(shorthand)*	youth	*(shorthand)*
your	*(shorthand)*	youthful	*(shorthand)*
you're	*(shorthand)*	Yule	*(shorthand)*
yours	*(shorthand)*	Yule-tide	*(shorthand)*

Z

zany	*(shorthand)*	zigzag	*(shorthand)*
zeal	*(shorthand)*	zinc	*(shorthand)*
zealot	*(shorthand)*	zipper	*(shorthand)*
zealous	*(shorthand)*	zither	*(shorthand)*
zebra	*(shorthand)*	zodiac	*(shorthand)*
zebu	*(shorthand)*	zollverein	*(shorthand)*
zenith	*(shorthand)*	zone	*(shorthand)*
zenon	*(shorthand)*	zoo	*(shorthand)*
zenophobia	*(shorthand)*	zoological	*(shorthand)*
zephyr	*(shorthand)*	zoologist	*(shorthand)*
Zeppelin	*(shorthand)*	zoology	*(shorthand)*
zero	*(shorthand)*	zoophyte	*(shorthand)*
zest	*(shorthand)*	zoophytic	*(shorthand)*

BRIEF FORMS

about	*ab*	at	*l*
above	*bv*	avoid	*avy*
absolute	*abs*	because	*ks*
acknowledge	*ak*	been	*b*
advantage	*avy*	begin	*bq*
advertise	*avy*	being	*b*
advice	*vrs*	beneficial	*bfx*
again	*ag*	benefit	*bnf*
against	*ag*	between	*bl*
allow	*le*	black	*b*
almost	*lro*	both	*bo*
already	*lr*	Britain	*B*
also	*lso*	British	*B*
always	*le*	business	*bs*
am	*⌒*	busy	*by*
America	*a*	but	*b*
American	*a*	buy	*b*
an	*a*	by	*b*
and	*+*	call	*kl*
appear	*ap*	came	*k*
approximate	*apx*	can	*k*
approximately	*apx*	charge	*cq*
around	*ru*	child	*u*
arrive	*rv*	children	*ul*
as	*as*	circumstance	*C,*
ask	*sk*	collect	*kk*

309

come	k	fine	f^u
coming	k	fire	fr
communicate	kuka	first	$f,$
country	K	for	f
day	d	full	fu
deal	dl	fully	fu
declare	dc	gentlemen	1
definite	dfn	girl	q
definitely	dfn	give	gu
deliver	dl	given	gu
delivery	dl	go	q
describe	des	God	Q
description	des	going	q
difficult	dfk	good	q
difficulty	dfk	great	q
during	du	had	h
east	ε	happen	hp
easy	eʒ	has	as
else	ls	have	v
equal	eq	having	v
equally	eq	he	h
establish	esl	held	hl
even	vn	help	hp
fail	fl	her	h
farm	f	him	⌒
feel	fl	his	s
field	fel	hole	hl
find	fi˙	hour	r

310

hundred		million	
idea		mine	
ignore		minimum	
importance		move	
important		necessarily	nec
in	n	necessary	nec
initial		newspaper	
intelligence		nice	ns
intelligent		north	
is		not	n
it		note	
keep	kp	object	ob
kind	ki	of	v
known	no	on	o
labour	lab	once	
large		only	nl
latter		open	op
learn	ln	opinion	opn
liberty	lb	opportunity	opl
life	lf	organization	og
like	lk	organize	og
line	li	ought	ol
little	ll	our	r
look	lo	out	ou
magazine		over	V
man		particular	P/
many		particularly	P/
market		peace	ps

piece	ps	self-explanatory	s/x
place	pl	several	sv
please	p	shall	ʒ
popular	pop	she	ʒ
price	ps	ship	ʒ
probable	pb	situation	sit
probably	pb	small	sma
prove	pv	south	S
public	pb	strength	S
publish	pb	subject	sj
pull	pu	succeed	suc
put	p	success	suc
question	q	successful	suc
real	rl	successfully	suc
really	rl	table	tab
regular	req	that	ta
regularly	req	the	•
remember	Rmb	their	ɿ
represent	rep	there	ɿ
representative	rep	they	ty
result	rsl	this	th
retain	rta	those	tos
room	rm	thought	tt
satisfaction	sat	thousand	T
satisfactory	sat	throughout	Tu
satisfy	sat	time	ti
save	sav	too	to
school	skl	turn	tn

until	*ul*	where	*ur*
up	*p*	while	*ul*
upon	*pn*	whole	*hl*
usual	*x*	whom	*hm*
usually	*x*	will	*l*
very	*v*	with	*⌣*
voice	*vy*	without	*⌣⌣*
war	*ur*	woman	*⌣⌐*
was	*η*	work	*uk*
we	*e*	world	*uo*
well	*l*	would	*d*
were	*⌣*	year	*y*
west	*∪*	your	*u*
what	*⌣a*		